T0289796

ROUTLEDGE LIBRARY EDITIONS:
ECONOMETRICS

Volume 7

INPUT/OUTPUT DATABASES

INPUT/OUTPUT DATABASES

Uses in Business and Government

JAY M. GOULD

Routledge
Taylor & Francis Group

LONDON AND NEW YORK

First published in 1979 by Garland

This edition first published in 2018
by Routledge
2 Park Square, Milton Park, Abingdon, Oxon OX14 4RN

and by Routledge
711 Third Avenue, New York, NY 10017

Routledge is an imprint of the Taylor & Francis Group, an informa business

© 1979 Garland STPM Press

British Library Cataloguing in Publication Data
A catalogue record for this book is available from the British Library

ISBN: 978-0-8153-9640-6 (Set)
ISBN: 978-1-351-14012-6 (Set) (ebk)
ISBN: 978-0-8153-5033-0 (Volume 7) (hbk)
ISBN: 978-1-351-14084-3 (Volume 7) (ebk)

Publisher's Note
The publisher has gone to great lengths to ensure the quality of this reprint but points out that some imperfections in the original copies may be apparent.

Disclaimer
The publisher has made every effort to trace copyright holders and would welcome correspondence from those they have been unable to trace.

input/output databases

databases

uses in business and government

jay m. gould

with a foreword by wassily leontief

garland stpm press/new york & london
an augustus m. kelley book

15 14 13 12 11 10 9 8 7 6 5 4 3 2 1

Library of Congress Cataloging in Publication Data

Gould, Jay M
    Input/output databases.

    "An Augustus M. Kelley book."
    Bibliography: p.
    Includes index.
    1. Electronic data processing. 2. Interindustry economics. 3. Management information systems.
    4. Planning—Data processing. 5. United States—Industries—Data processing. I. Title.
    HF5548.2.G634   658.4′03   78-14084
    ISBN 0-8240-7058-5

foreword

This volume introduces the reader to a relatively little known sector of the modern data processing industry. Independent computerized data banks play an ever increasing role in the modern information revolution. They already have markedly affected decision-making in government and in economics. It is high time that academic researchers and teachers, along with professional economists, executives, students, government administrators, data processing managers, business librarians, and even lawyers all become aware of these new rich and versatile sources of comprehensive and detailed factual economic information.

Dr. Jay M. Gould, the organizer of the first successful private input/output data bank, describes its present and prospective uses with authoritative knowledge and great enthusiasm. The ability to identify key participants in the market place represents an important private sector contribution to public information.

—Wassily Leontief

preface

In 1975, the United States Senate Committee on Interior and Insular Affairs held hearings on a National Energy Information Act, in the course of which I was asked to submit a statement on the role that input/output databases could play in the establishment of such an information system. I was asked to do so as president of a private firm, Economic Information Systems, Inc., (EIS) which had developed a Fuel and Energy Database for the Federal Energy Administration, and similar databases for the Federal Trade Commission, the Department of Justice, and the Federal Preparedness Agency. Questions raised by Senator Floyd Haskell of Colorado at the hearings suggested that there may be a broader interest in this subject than that of the immediate users of the EIS databases in government and business, who are provided with technical manuals to guide their access to the database.

In preparing these chapters for that broader audience, I have therefore tried to avoid technical terms as much as possible. Readers should know, however, that the term "input/output database" as used here refers to an information system, in machine-readable form, carrying estimates on the intermediate consumption of a given commodity or service by those specified firms accounting for the bulk of such consumption. I have tried to describe in these chapters how such databases can be constructed from publicly available data, their characteristics and uses in economic and marketing analysis, and how they can serve as components in large-scale input/output models that can simulate the transactions of the United States economy, and to illuminate specific problems in corporate, regional, and national economic planning.

contents

chapter 1

input/output analysis and its background

The analytical power of input/output economics, for which its inventor, Wassily Leontief, was awarded the Nobel Prize in 1973, has yet to achieve the recognition it deserves among American economists. Aside from a small group of his disciples who teach at perhaps two dozen American universities, there are all too few courses in input/output analysis offered in the United States today. While most of the pioneer work in the theory and construction of input/output tables has been done by Leontief at Harvard, by Anne Carter at Brandeis, and by a dedicated group of government input/output technicians centered in Washington, D.C., the bulk of the well-earned plaudits for input/output has come from abroad. Input/output tables make up the underlying core of the national income accounts and planning programs for most of the nations of the world today, for which statistical standards are set by the United Nations.

In an effort to help encourage the use of input/output methodology here, I have addressed these chapters to economists, students, government administrators, business executives, environmentalists, and others who I think will see in input/output a method to analyze such problems as inflation, energy and transportation requirements, and environmental pollution.

All this suggests, of course, that input/output is a par excellence tool for planning at the national, regional, and corporate level. It is the past association with national economic planning that has aroused some suspicion and even hostility toward Leontief's work. Let me, therefore, attempt a brief and nontechnical review of the theory and development of input/output analysis, from the vantage of one of the few economists who has had sufficient professional involvement with input/output to appreciate its power as an analytic tool and its potential for illuminating problems of economic policy. (There are many detailed expositions of input/output economics available both to the lay reader and to professional economists. See Bibliography in Appendix A.)

Input/output is not a body of economic doctrine but a way of seeing how the interrelationships of an economic system can be represented in a two-dimensional model that traces the output (or sales) of each economic sector to all other sectors. In an input/output table, each sector or industry is arrayed both horizontally (as sellers) and vertically (as buyers). Transactions between selling and buying industries can be viewed in two ways. Each row indicates the sales or deliveries of the selling industry and each column records the purchase or inputs of the buying industry. The degree of interdependence of the various industries can be measured by the buy-sell transactions that appear in each cell formed by the intersection of a row and a column.

This view of the interdependence of economic sectors can be traced back to Quesnay's *Tableau Economique* (1759), and has reappeared in the work of many economists since. In the 1880s, Leon Walras elaborated the concept, as a purely theoretical abstraction, as a set of mathematical equations that related the prices and quantities of all commodities produced by society.

It occurred to Leontief, in 1931 when he was twenty-five years of age, that with the help of statistical data such equations could be made to represent the sectors that define an economic system in equilibrium, in which all outputs equal all inputs into the system. Such equations could then yield a simultaneous solution that would measure the degree of interdependence of all the economic sectors that make up the system. But such input/output tables required massive collections of detailed statistical data of a quality then available only in the United States. In 1931, in response to an invitation from Wesley C. Mitchell of the National Bureau of Economic Research, Leontief came to the United States, after doing his graduate work at the University of Leningrad and after several productive years at the Institute of World Economics in Kiel. Moving on to Harvard in 1932, and with the help of a Rockefeller grant and a graduate assistant, he began the construction of the first input/output tables based on U.S. Census data for the years 1919 and 1929.

With the onset of World War II, the Bureau of Labor Statistics financed the extension of the tables to 1939. These tables, which were completed in 1941, proved very useful to government economists, particularly in the later years of the war when postwar reconversion problems arose. In 1944, for example, two BLS economists, W. Duane Evans and Marvin Hoffenberg, used a 95 sector breakdown of the 1939 tables to predict that postwar demands on the economy would require nearly 100 million tons of steel capacity. Although regarded with skepticism by some steel executives, this figure was attained by 1950.

In the wake of this successful wartime experience, the Bureau of Labor Statistics launched the second full-scale government-sponsored input/output study. With a budget of $1.5 million provided by the Air Force, several dozen professional economists and statisticians worked for five years in the preparation of input/output tables for the Census benchmark year of 1947. These were the first detailed input/output tables, which, based on a breakdown of the U.S. economy into 200 sectors, required the newly invented high-speed computer to solve the equations that measured the degree of interdependence of all 200 sectors.

The results of this study were released in the early 1950s, at a time when political attitudes to "planning" had changed. The authors of the 1947 input/output study were undoubtedly surprised to find some economists attacking the study as "socialistic," while others attacked it on technical grounds. The Eisenhower Administration suspended input/output research, ironically, just after the death of Stalin, when the Soviet Union lifted its own ban on input/output research.

Government support for input/output was restored in the Kennedy Administration, and the technique has since gained steady acceptance. Input/output tables for 1967 and 1972, prepared by economists in the Bureau of Economic Analysis of the Department of Commerce, measure the requirements, on both current and capital account, for more than 600 sectors. Economists can use these and similar tables stored in a computer memory to evaluate within minutes the impact on the total economy of any assumed set of economic shifts.

I first became acquainted with input/output in the late 1930s when I came to the National Bureau of Economic Research to do my graduate work in the analysis of productivity trends. Leontief had long since left the National Bureau, but publication of his preliminary findings in 1936 and 1937 had stirred great interest, particularly among the younger research associates.* I was especially impressed with the simplicity with which the changes in the "technical coefficients" (indicated by the transactions in each cell) could be taken to define the degree of technological advance of an economy, so important in the explanation of productivity gains. I followed closely the subsequent development of input/output research and found it useful in my own work as a business consultant in the postwar years.

In 1952, I became interested in the fact that entries to be found along each row of the 1947 tables could be used by industrial marketing analysts to evaluate markets for the goods produced by the row sector. To the extent that entries in each cell reflected the realities of the marketplace, I began to speculate on whether it would be possible to identify the participants in these market transactions. To my surprise, I found this to be rather easy because most markets were dominated by a relatively small number of large enterprises. I then worked out a procedure to estimate market shares by relating the reported sales of particular companies to "universe" estimates taken from Census and input/output tables.

Of particular use in antitrust litigation, these procedures received high judicial sanction when the Supreme Court, in 1958, upheld a lower court ruling in the Brown Shoe Case, for which I had been retained by the Anti-Trust Division of the Department of Justice to prepare estimates of market shares. After several dozen similarly successful antitrust applications, I realized that there was an enormous store of public information available about the operations of large companies, and that if it were possible to standardize this information to fit the input/output tables, the informational content of the tables would expand enormously.

In 1966, I established a company called Economic Information Systems (EIS) and was retained by the IBM Company in a three-way joint arrangement with the Dun and Bradstreet Company to develop an "input/output data bank." The Dun and Bradstreet establishment information, based on credit ratings, turned out to be too heavily oriented to small firms whose financial status was in doubt. In 1969, I and my associate, Bentley H. Paykin, set out to

---

*Robert Dorfman has described the excitement created by those early papers as follows: "The Walrasian general equilibrium theory was a scheme of economic interconnections in principle, which might be implemented in some future, visionary stage of the development of the science. With Leontief's papers that higher, more competent stage arrived abruptly. The time-honored theory was lifted suddenly out of the textbooks and treatises and placed in the arena of applied economic analysis." ("Wassily Leontief's Contribution to Economics," *Swedish Journal of Economics,* Vol. 75, 1973, pp. 430-449)

develop a database restricted to business establishments with more than twenty employees that would have a sufficient degree of accuracy to match the input/output tables. That task has now been completed. EIS input/output databases are widely used today both by the business community and by government agencies.

In the chapters that follow I will explore some of the larger issues involved in this widespread use of input/output tables to reflect the realities of the marketplace. In reviewing the history of those input/output applications, three themes will be developed in detail, which merit a summary statement at the outset.

First, one of the great merits of input/output analysis is that it can redirect the attention of economists from macro- to micro-levels of analysis and particularly to the relationship of technology to economic advance. We are emerging from a long period in which our national economic policy could be compared to driving a car—with fiscal and tax policy serving as the brake and gas pedal. Having achieved both inflation and high unemployment, we must now lift the hood to see how the engine really works, a task for which input/output analysis is a crucial diagnostic tool.

Second, the use of input/output analysis for national economic planning (as opposed to corporate planning) is still a highly controversial issue, although academic criticism on technical grounds is no longer as vocal as it was twenty years ago. I believe that political objections are irrelevant to any evaluation of what is really a tool of analysis rather than a body of doctrine. Nevertheless, there are political objections to the association of input/output with national planning by those who object to the latter as interference with the free play of market forces. Since the federal government has long been engaged in such intervention on a massive scale, the true issues should not be government intervention as such, but rather what kind, to what ends, and with what means. Public debate on recent National Planning Bills should center on these questions, which will be discussed in the final chapters.

Opponents of national planning do strike a sensitive nerve in their warnings of the danger of overcentralization. Thomas A. Murphy, Chairman of General Motors, in his criticism of an early version of the Humphrey-Hawkins Bill, stated:

The bill carries implications which are a serious threat to the welfare and freedom of our citizens and to the continued dynamic development of our national economy.

The bill seems to proceed upon the erroneous assumption that given sufficient economic information and access to public opinion, a central group can decide on appropriate priorities for the entire economy. In reality, it is impossible to make such judgments on the optimal employment of society's resources. (*N.Y. Sunday Times,* Dec. 21, 1975)

In wartime of course, a central group, namely the President and his advisers, do indeed decide on appropriate priorities for the entire economy, but Mr. Murphy is quite right that such a politically acceptable consensus has never been reached in our history in peacetime.

Nevertheless, I believe that Mr. Murphy is fighting a straw man. No believer in a democratic system would accept national planning if it meant according great power over investment decisions to a small group of persons. A democratic National Plan would require an information feedback system that would permit the participation of many diverse groups in those decisions. A national economic plan should therefore require publication of detailed projections for all economic sectors and one that should be read and debated by all who would be affected by those projections. National planning in a democracy should involve first and foremost a gigantic sharing of *information,* as against current practice where some of the most crucial decisions affecting our economic destiny are made in the boardrooms of giant companies or by government agencies with access to limited data.

The third and key question has to do with the flow of information in a democratic society. Questions about the control of information have come to the fore as subjects of national interest in recent years for two principal reasons: the emergence of the computer as an awesome instrument for the centralization of information, with its potential abuse by both government and business, and the continued concentration of key information in relatively few private hands. It is important, therefore, that some momentous questions about the role of information in a democratic society be touched upon: the rights of individuals as natural persons to privacy; the rights of companies to corporate secrecy; and the rights of persons and companies to access to government information, as embodied in recent Freedom of Information and "Sunshine" legislation.

In our free-enterprise system a necessary distinction must be made between public information and the private information deemed necessarily confidential to ensure the viability and profitable operation of the individual firm. When such information is reported to Census or tax agencies, by law it can be released publicly only in the form of statistical aggregates in which no single firm is identified. Input/output models are constructed by assembling hundreds of thousands of such statistical aggregates, which by themselves do not identify individual firms.

It is my belief that a privately assembled input/output database, in which the statistical aggregates used to construct input/output models are allocated to specific firms on the basis of public records, does not violate the tradition of confidentiality so necessary for the collection of accurate Census data, on which all planning decisions, both private and public, must be based. Because such databases are available to the public, they can facilitate an informed public debate in which, for example, the impact of economic decisions made by government agencies or by large enterprises can be systematically and objectively examined, with realistic appraisals of magnitude, and without invading the privacy of any one firm since all the data would be inferences based on public records.

It is important to examine how these input/output databases can be constructed, how they can be used, and the implications of their use by business and government. Since I am functioning in a dual capacity, both as an input/output specialist and also as head of a firm that sells such databases as a professional service, I am aware that the claims I shall make for such databases may be regarded as self-serving and promotional, particularly since all the examples and most of the tabular material shown here are taken directly from the records and experience of my firm, Economic Information Systems, Inc., which since 1970 has developed scores of input/output databases and remains the only firm that offers such a service.* With such a warning of possible bias on my part, I shall have to let the reader make his own judgment on this score.

It may be helpful at this juncture to describe a typical input/output database in general terms before addressing the technical details of its construction and use, as is done in Chapters 2 and 3. There is one we can discuss because it involves a public institution.

The United States Postal Service has made use of a specially prepared Database of Package Mailers, which physically consists

* A partial list of companies and agencies for whom EIS has prepared input/output databases includes: A. E. Staley, Acco, Airco, Allied Chemical, American Standard, Atlantic Richfield, Bellows International, Bridgeport Brass, Champion International, Cincinnati Milacron, Combustion Engineering, Container Corporation of America, Consolidated Freightways, Continental Corrugated, Crown Zellerbach, Curtiss 1000, Dart Industries, De Laval Separator, Diamond Crystal Salt, Dow Chemical, Dresser Industries, E. I. duPont, Eaton, FMC, Federal Energy Administration, Federal Preparedness Agency, Federal Trade Commission, Flying Tiger, Frontier Airlines, Garlock, General Tire, Getty, Glidden–Durkee, Goodyear Tire, Great Plains Bag, Gulf Oil, Information Handling, Inland Container, Inmont, International Correspondence Schools, International Paper, ITT Grinnell, Mark Controls, Markem, Marlin Rockwell, Menasha, Mobil Oil, Monsanto, North American Van Lines, Norton, NL Industries, Olin, Parker Packing, Pillsbury, Potlatch, Ralston Purina, Sandvik, Soabar, Sperry Vickers, Stelco, Sun Oil, Texaco, U.S. Corrugated, U.S. Department of Justice, U.S. Postal Service, U.S. Plywood, U.S. Steel, Union Camp, Union Carbide, Uniroyal, United Parcel Service, Vulcan Materials, Westvaco, Weyerhaeuser.

of a reel of magnetic tape that identifies some 100,000 business establishments, which as a group mail or otherwise ship about 1.5 billion packages annually.

The Postal Service is in the unusual position of a public institution with a mandate from Congress to achieve the efficiencies of operation of a private firm. Although a government parcel post service can be traced back to colonial days, in recent decades private companies have proved to be viable competitors for the delivery of small packages. Thus, the Postal Service finds itself no longer in a monopoly situation, and is now required to evaluate its position in this market and to seek to extend its current market share. To do this, the Postal Service, as would any other non-monopolist, would first have to identify all the components of this market and to ascertain what part of the market it currently holds. These are questions that cannot be answered by the Postal Service, but can be answered by a Database of Package Mailers, the construction of which rests on two major sets of inferences.

The first is the ability of input/output research techniques to discern that the major package mailers are those industries typically shipping products of relatively high value but small bulk and this relationship can be quantified. It thus becomes possible to select (and quantify) about 200 such industries, including mail-order houses, department stores, publishers, manufacturers of electronics, machinery parts, etc. The second inference is to assume that within each of these 200 industries, each establishment operates in a similar fashion except for the factor of size. Thus, a mail-order house that is twice the size of another will typically mail twice as many packages. As Chapters 2 and 3 indicate, these inferences are close enough to the realities of the marketplace to permit a company to select a relatively small number of locations accounting for the bulk of its total market, and then go on to secure from that small sample the information necessary to guide its strategy in enlarging its market share. I am, of course, summarizing a set of procedures that in practice amounts to a highly systematic and ongoing search for new customers, but one that offers immediate bottomline rewards.

I have chosen package mailing for illustration, because it is a common, familiar service and requires no special technological understanding. Nevertheless, the degree to which various industries are dependent on package mailing rests on technological factors familiar to all input/output statisticians. Similar technological factors, however, will be reflected in the sales experience of every firm that sells products or services to other firms. Therefore, the insights available from input/output databases are available to all companies, large and small, that will take the trouble to investigate this new facility. This means, in effect, that all companies serving intermediate markets (i.e., that sell to other firms) now have the ability, at least in theory, to obtain a complete understanding of their relative position in the markets they serve, and to extend their customer base wherever they choose.

It does not mean, however, that if all companies choose to avail themselves of this facility, the benefits to all will be self-canceling. There will remain a host of diverse factors that will cause two competing companies to respond differently to similar situations. For example, one sales manager, on learning that he has a very low market share in any one area or industry, may conclude that the marginal return on additional sales and promotional investment might be higher in other markets in which he faces less resistance. Others may choose to emphasize a long-run investment strategy to ensure a more balanced representation in all markets.

On balance, it is clear that a company making use of an input/output database identifying all of its potential customers can greatly increase the productivity of its sales force. In this way the extended use of input/output databases can help expand sales and output, and at the same time serve as an aid to competition. Chapters 2 and 3 will help the reader appraise the value of input/output databases in the private sector. Chapters 4 and 5 will examine the use of such databases in illuminating broader public sector problems of national and regional policy.

chapter 2 a database of u.s. business enterprise

The Database of Business Enterprise is a file of machine-readable records containing two types of information about U.S. business establishments. The *basic* portion of the record contains publicly available information about the establishment, such as its name, address, telephone number, employment, industry, and parent company (if any). In addition to the "public domain" information, each record can include one or more *inferential* items of information about that establishment based on input/output calculations. The great efficiency of input/output as a mode of storing and "creating" information is indicated by the fact that as many as 1,000 different items of information about each establishment can be calculated from a highly detailed input/output matrix. These calculations result from computer programs that link two files.

The first file stores the basic—i.e., public—information about each business establishment, and the second file is a rectangular input/output matrix of current direct transactions, tracing the deliveries of about 1,000 goods and services to about 700 industries. Thus, the input/output matrix can be visualized as containing 700,000 cells in a two-dimensional grid pattern.

the database of business enterprise

We have found it possible to distill from various published sources nearly 350,000 records covering the "universe" of all business establishments with twenty or more employees, coded by industry, and accounting for the employment of about 40 million persons and sales of $2.9 trillion for the year 1976. Before describing how this file was created and how it is maintained, a necessary technical definition must be made, following Census Bureau usage, of the difference between an establishment and an enterprise.

An establishment is an economic unit, generally at a single physical location, whose primary activity can be designated by a 4-digit Standard Industrial Classification (SIC) code. The Census Bureau has defined about 700 different industries ranging from agriculture to government. Thus, an establishment can be a farm, mine, plant, warehouse, store, or office location.

An enterprise or company is a legal entity that can own or control one or more business establishments. A company can carry a numeric *company* code (which will also be carried by all its establishments) but can carry a SIC code only if, at the same address, some business activity is conducted other than central administrative functions. Historically, companies evolved from single establishments having a primary activity in a single industry, but today large multiplant companies typically operate establishments in several industries.

public information sources

What is the source of "public" information? The public records consist of information published in a variety of ways. A record can appear initially as a name, address, and telephone number in the classified section of a telephone book, which offers, incidentally, a very useful way of assigning SIC codes. Additional information may be found in state or industrial directories or in the business press. There is a large body of information available about all public and private companies reporting to various regulatory agencies. Possibly the most significant source of information comes from annual reports, available for about 10,000 public companies.

An additional invaluable information resource is the statistical tabulations of the Census Bureau, which offer the crucial "controls" that serve as indicators of database accuracy. For example, an annual publication of the Department of Commerce, *County Business Patterns,* indicates how many establishments fall into each 4-digit industry in each state and county and in each of ten different employment size classes. Annual issues of this publication are compared with corresponding entries in the EIS file, in order to focus on divergences.

The technology of compiling published information in database form was developed in recent years in the mailing list industry. Today, for example, with the use of optical scanning techniques, the cost of putting a record (consisting of a name and an address, plus additional items) into machine-readable form is little more than the cost of typing an address label. But a database is far more than a computerized mailing list, and its creation requires the successful matching of identical records from different databases in order that all the information available in each database can be associated with the correct record. Sophisticated computer programs are now available that can match identical records despite the great variations in spelling or nomenclature that characterize the way a particular firm or establishment may be listed in public documents.

These matching programs are facilitated by the use of a laboriously compiled "parent-child" reference file that carries the name of the "parent" for about 150,000 branch and subsidiary locations of multiestablishment companies. This enables the computer to recognize as General Motors locations such names as Chevrolet, Buick, Allison-Diesel, etc. This file is updated periodically to take into account recent mergers and acquisitions.

The ability to match one database with another facilitates computerized information exchanges, which lie at the heart of database development. EIS has made such exchange arrangements with most of its clients including several publishers of trade magazines and two large mailing list houses. In addition, the EIS file is periodically matched against customer files of large companies that wish to transfer to their customer prospects information from the EIS file. All records in the customer list *not* matched to the EIS file are clerically reviewed and are added to the EIS file when validated. Circulation and mailing lists of business firms can in this way benefit from the Database ability to analyze the coverage of these files by industry, employment, or size of sales, while the coverage of the Database benefits from the high degree of currency inherent in a circulation, subscription, or customer file.

This ability to match two computer files to transfer data from one to the other has also raised some troublesome issues about the invasion of privacy. It should be stressed that we are dealing here with public information, and with public information about companies and not about individuals, which is a key difference. Although corporations may want to be regarded as persons under the 14th Amendment, Congress and the courts have not in recent years accorded to companies the same privacy rights that individuals have under the Constitution. In fact, recent Freedom of Information legislation now often facilitates the process of securing information about firms in industries regulated by government agencies.

Public concern about privacy of information has evolved in recent years with the development of the computer and the ease with which matching programs can facilitate the transfer of information from one database to another. Whether the database owner be a government agency, a bank, or an insurance company, for example, the opportunities for abuse are readily apparent and remain an unresolved problem. But one useful principle has evolved, which requires full disclosure to a person from the database owner of any information contained therein about that person, so that erroneous information can be changed. The Fair Credit Reporting Act requires credit-rating services to report to any inquiring individual the information carried about that person. While companies cannot claim the same right as persons, the same principle can apply to business databases. The EIS Database is in fact accessible to anyone, including the firms covered.

In any case, since EIS information comes from public records, a company cannot lay claim to an invasion of privacy concerning any information about that firm in the Database. Actually, large public companies increasingly recognize a need, continually expressed in annual reports, to disclose more rather than less information about company operations. Perhaps this acknowledges a concern about a possible gulf between the realities of corporate power and the legitimization of the uses of that power in the eyes of society. At any rate, it has now become somewhat easier to secure data about company activities from materials released by the company itself.

The coverage and accuracy of the EIS file is enhanced by its increasing exposure to public use by way of timesharing services. Since 1975, online public access to the file has been provided by the Lockheed Information Retrieval Service, a subsidiary of Lockheed Aircraft, with a telephone-linked terminal network available twenty hours a day anywhere in the United States, Western Europe, and Japan. The Lockheed system enables the EIS Database to function as an instantaneous national telephone directory, and a national business and financial directory.

In 1978, the EIS file became available to online users of two additional timesharing networks—the TRW Business Credit Division offers EIS information through terminals to members of the National Association of Credit Management, and the Cybernet Division of Control Data Corporation now offers computational access to EIS data in machine readable form to corporate analysts.

characteristics of the eis database of business enterprise

The EIS Database does not purport to offer complete coverage of the U.S. economy. While deliberately modeled on the Census Bureau publication *County Business Patterns,* the Database excludes all small establishments, all government and many non-profit sectors, as well as certain private sectors that are not characterized by corporate modes of organization, such as farming and medical and health services. Banks are also excluded because they merit separate treatment accorded to them in financial databases available elsewhere. The EIS file is a database of *corporate* enterprise. Unlike the reports of government agencies that generally by law cannot permit the identification of individual enterprises, the database can report on "who is who" and thereby afford more revealing insights into the corporate structure of the U.S. economy.

In Table 2–1, the salient statistics are offered for the Database for the year 1976, in terms of the coverage of establishments,

table 2–1
characteristics of the eis database of business enterprise, 1976

	Approximate Number of Firms (thousands)	Number of Establishments (thousands)	Sales ($ Billion)	Employment (thousands)	Total Private Employment (thousands)	Employment Coverage Ratio
Mining	2.0	5.5	65.1	400	600	66
Construction	22.0	23.1	78.0	2,020	3,594	56
Manufacturing	73.8	121.0	1,159.1	18,850	19,600	96
Transportation	10.0	11.3	80.3	2,065 }	4,509	75
Utilities	4.2	5.3	110.2	1,330 }		
Wholesale Trade	44.0	59.3	566.2	2,460	4,263	58
Retail Trade	35.0	63.7	284.0	4,420	13,431	33
Finance, mainly Insurance (excluding Banks)	.8	1.0	134.3	4,100	4,316	94
Services (Agriculture, etc.)	33.2	71.0	70.1	4,802	14,824	33
Total	**225.0**	**361.2**	**2,547.3**	**40,447**	**63,137**	**62**

The 225,000 firms in the EIS Database of Business Enterprise shown here account for over 40 million employees and about $3 trillion of sales, including those of foreign subsidiaries. The omission of government, nonprofit sectors, and nonincorporated agriculture, retail, and service industries brings the total employment coverage down to 62%. The corporate sectors of the economy, however, especially in manufacturing, have extremely high coverage, on the order of 75%–95%.

employment, and sales volume. For the year 1976, the Database included 225,000 firms, operating 361,000 establishments with twenty or more employees, accounting for some $2.6 trillion of domestic sales. They employed 40.4 million persons, accounting for 62% of total private employment in 1976, with varying degrees of coverage by sector, corresponding to the degree to which each sector is characterized by corporate organization. Coverage is highest in manufacturing, and lowest in the service and agricultural sectors.

concentration of american business enterprise

One of the most striking characteristics of the American business enterprise structure is corporate concentration, or the dominant position of a relatively small number of firms in most markets. That concentration represents the reality of the marketplace is attested to by the publication, since 1947, of Census Bureau "concentration ratios" in each industry, supplemented by the industrial marketing rule of thumb that "80% of your business will come from 20% of your customers."* With variations depending on the particular market, database studies have also demonstrated the essential validity of concentration for hundreds of products and industries.

While the Census Bureau traces changes in the statistical magnitude of concentration in various manufacturing industries, the EIS Database offers some new details on the precise degree of American business concentration, both in manufacturing and in all other business sectors.

Official measures of aggregate concentration in manufacturing come from the Census Bureau, but are confined to the top 200 firms, which in the 1972 Census of Manufactures were found to account for 42% of total value-added and 43% of total shipments. Previous Census data indicate a fairly steady upward progression in the value-added percentage of the top 200 manufacturing companies since 1947, when the percentage stood at 30. Other official measures of concentration for the top 200 manufacturing companies indicate that in 1973 their share of total assets and profits was even higher (65%), because of their higher share of capital investment.†

The Database offers an opportunity to define the degree of concentration in American business on a broader basis. It would

*Cf. U.S. Census Bureau, Census of Manufactures, 1972, "Concentration Ratios in Manufacturing" MC72(SR)-2.

† For example, the top 200 manufacturing firms reported 51% of total new capital expenditures in the 1972 Census of Manufactures.

be a crude oversimplification to infer on the basis of Census Bureau evidence on the dominant position of the top 200 companies that concentration stops at that level.

For the past fifteen years, *Fortune* magazine has published annual statistical compendiums of the top 500 "industrials," and in more recent years has added data for an additional 500 industrial and 250 nonindustrial firms. But the *Fortune* sales data, as compared with Database sales data, overestimate the degree of concentration achieved by these companies in domestic markets, because of the inclusion of sales of foreign subsidiaries.

The EIS Database allocates sales of large firms to all domestic establishments in both manufacturing and nonmanufacturing industries, with an independent estimate for sales of foreign subsidiaries. Table 2–2 offers a sales breakdown for the year 1976 for

table 2–2
breakdown of sales for top companies in eis database, 1976

Leading Number of Companies	Cumulated Total Number of Employees (millions)	Cumulated Sales Volume ($ billion)			
		Manufacturing	Non-Manufacturing	Foreign	Total
200	9.7	390.4	389.9	229.3	1,009.7
500	14.7	530.1	552.5	268.2	1,350.9
1,000	18.7	623.0	687.6	288.5	1,599.2
1,500	20.9	675.1	756.9	296.8	1,728.8
2,000	22.3	704.7	806.6	300.5	1,811.7
2,500	23.3	729.7	839.4	302.6	1,871.6
3,000	24.1	747.2	867.4	303.6	1,918.2
3,500	24.8	763.6	888.4	304.0	1,956.0
4,000	25.3	775.3	908.2	304.3	1,987.8
4,500	25.8	788.5	922.5	304.6	2,015.5
5,000	26.2	798.5	936.7	304.7	2,039.9
10,000	28.7	866.5	1,021.4	305.1	2,193.0
20,000	30.8	925.6	1,116.9	305.1	2,347.7
30,000	32.5	980.8	1,157.5	305.2	2,443.4
40,000	33.5	1,006.0	1,201.0	305.2	2,512.2
50,000	34.4	1,033.7	1,228.6	305.2	2,567.5
All Other 173,583	6.0	125.7	213.2	.0	338.9
Total, all firms 223,583	**40.4**	**1,159.4**	**1,441.9**	**305.2**	**2,960.4**

This table reveals concentration patterns among the firms in the EIS Database. The top 500, which differ from the "*Fortune* 500" only in the inclusion of several dozen or so large private firms in both the industrial and nonindustrial sectors, are seen to account for a sales volume of $1.4 trillion out of a total of $3 trillion, or about 47%. The top 50,000 firms will increase sales coverage to $2.6 trillion or to 87% of the corporate total.

the top 50,000 companies (with respect to total sales volume), a breakdown never before available from any source.*

The top 50,000 firms appear to account for 85.2% of total domestic sales in the indicated private sectors. Since these firms represent less than 1% of all business enterprises, this figure is itself a measure of market concentration.

Table 2–2 indicates that the top 2,500 companies account for $1.6 trillion or nearly 60% of total domestic sales and for 63% of total manufacturing sales. Note that Table 4–1 indicates what proportion of total sales is accounted for within each 2-digit SIC sector. It is clear that in most sectors, except for farming and some of the retail trades and service sectors, these top 2,500 companies (constituting companies with more than 1,000 employees, and at least $50 million of sales) do indeed account for more than half of total sales in most markets.

Perhaps the most succinct measure of corporate concentration in the American economy is the fact indicated by Table 2–2, that the top 1,000 firms in 1976 accounted for $1.6 trillion or 54% of total corporate sales including those of foreign subsidiaries. In terms of domestic sales, they accounted for $1.3 trillion or 49.3% of the corporate total.[†]

It is interesting to note that such figures were not available to the Cost of Living Council when it monitored the sales of large firms in the closing years of the first Nixon Administration. Council statisticians established a four-tier system to assign relative importance to large companies, but were uncertain as to where to draw the line in order to minimize the number of significant returns to be examined. Table 4–1 suggests that the top 2,500 may have been a suitable number, for half of the sales volume of most markets would then be accounted for.

---

*Corporate concentration statistics are also available from tabulations prepared annually by the Bureau of Internal Revenue, and by the Federal Trade Commission, but are reported only for several hundred companies with asset values in the ranges of $100 million to $250 million; $250 million to $1 billion; and over $1 billion.

[†]This is astonishingly close to John Kenneth Galbraith's speculation that "In the United States one may think of one thousand manufacturing, merchandising, transportation, power and financial corporations producing approximately half of all the goods and services not provided by the state." (John Kenneth Galbraith, *Economics and the Public Purpose,* Boston: Houghton Mifflin, 1973, p. 42.) Galbraith considers that by virtue of their superior size, market power, and ability to create the new technology necessary to sustain their dominant shares of the market, these companies constitute a "planning" sector, in contrast to the millions of other enterprises that must live or die according to the "free" play of market forces. Therefore, Galbraith suggests, if inflationary forces get strong enough to require federal wage and price controls, the number of separate companies that would have to be monitored to achieve effective regulation is quite small.

database coverage

In Chapter 4 we shall consider other measures of concentration and offer some insights in the analysis of concentration available from the Database. Because corporate concentration represents a reality of the marketplace, the huge volume of information publicly available about large public and private companies ensures high coverage with respect to sales. For example, there are about 10,000 public companies reporting to the SEC that must disclose their sales volume and other pertinent information each year by law. Of these, the top 3,000 account for more than 70% of total corporate sales, and for these companies, on whom is focused the full attention of the financial and business press of the country, Database coverage is practically complete—certainly at the 99% level.

Somewhat equivalent coverage is achieved for large private companies, which by virtue of their size cannot keep their existence unknown, although the degree of accuracy with which their sales volume can be estimated falls below that of public companies. Nevertheless, for companies both public and private with sales of $25 million or more, Database coverage is probably well above 95%.

At the lower end of the scale—firms or establishments with sales ranging in the area of $0.5 million to $5 million—EIS coverage may be no better than 75%. Since establishments and firms with fewer than twenty employees account for less than 5% of total sales volume, we do not feel that unit coverage deficiencies at the low end of the scale will significantly decrease the percentages of total corporate sales accounted for by the firms in the Database.

Table 2–3 lists 43 private companies and subsidiaries of foreign companies that were large enough in 1975 (with sales volume exceeding $300 million) to have been included in the 1976 "Fortune 500," but were not because the Fortune list is restricted to public companies. Because of their size, however, their activities were well reported in the business press, and hence they found their way into the Database with whatever degree of accuracy had been attained by the various published news stories. Probably the one private company subject to the heaviest press scrutiny, or speculation, is Hughes Aircraft (or better still its then parent, Summa Corporation) precisely because so much of its operations were deliberately cloaked in secrecy. Nevertheless, the fact that Hughes Aircraft has thousands of employees and well-publicized government contracts could not itself be concealed from public view.

In the aggregate the economic importance of these enterprises (with $39 billion of sales) has probably been overlooked because

table 2–3
nonpublic companies with sales over $300 million in 1975 not carried in *fortune* 500 list

Company Name	Headquarters City	State	Sales ($ Million)
A. W. Perdue & Sons	Salisbury	Md.	300
Allen-Bradley	Milwaukee	Wisc.	300
American Hoechst	New York	N.Y.	620
Basf Corp	Charlotte	N.Ca.	590
Cargill	Minneapolis	Minn.	10800
Carling O'Keefe Ltd.	Toronto	Ont.	300
Ciba-Geigy	Ardsley	N.Y.	860
Continental Grain	New York	N.Y.	6000
Deering Milliken	New York	N.Y.	1100
Dubuque Packing	Dubuque	Iowa	550
E & J Gallo Winery	Modesto	Calif.	400
Estee Lauder	New York	N.Y.	375
Farmers Union Central Exchange	St. Paul	Minn.	500
Farmers Union Grain Terminal	St. Paul	Minn.	1260
Field Enterprises	Chicago	Ill.	425
Gates Rubber Co.	Denver	Colo.	700
H. P. Hood & Sons	Boston	Mass.	430
Hallmark	Kansas City	Mo.	500
Hearst Co.	New York	N.Y.	375
Hoffman–La Roche	Nutley	N.J.	700
Hughes Aircraft	Culver City	Calif.	1600
Hunt Oil	Dallas	Tx.	500
ICI United States	Wilmington	Del.	300
J. R. Simplot	Boise	Idaho	350
Lennox Industries	Marshalltown	Iowa	300
Leviton Mfg. Co.	Little Neck	N.Y.	300
Mars Inc.	Mc Lean	Va.	750
Mid–American Dairymen	Springfield	Mo.	635
Mobay Chemical	Pittsburgh	Pa.	500
Moore Business Forms	Niagara Falls	N.Y.	635
Moorman Mfg. Co.	Quincy	Ill.	300
National Beef Packing	Kansas City	Ks.	350
Readers Digest	Pleasantville	N.Y.	800
S. C. Johnson & Son	Racine	Wisc.	600
S. I. Newhouse, Advance Publ.	Staten Island	N.Y.	800
Southern States Coop	Richmond	Va.	300
Southwire Co.	Lubbock	Tx.	300
Stroh Brewery	Detroit	Mich.	300
Sunkist Growers Inc.	Sherman Oaks	Calif.	450
Simpson Timber Co.	Seattle	Wash.	300
Timex Corp.	Middlebury	Conn.	350
Triangle Publications	Radnor	Pa.	300
Tribune Co.	Chicago	Ill.	700
		Total Sales	**39005**

of their nonpublic status. There is some evidence that large private companies have been growing in importance in recent years. Companies like Cargill and Continental Grain operate in wholesale grain markets where speed and flexibility enjoyed by privately owned firms offer advantages over their public counterparts. In recent years some public companies have found their opportunities for expansion limited by low price/earnings ratios and have been reported as actively buying up their own stock in an effort to become private firms. There also appears to be above-average growth in the operations of American subsidiaries of foreign companies like Ciba–Geigy and Hoffman–La Roche, which do not need to report to the SEC.

The degree of coverage of firms in the Database varies of course with the size of the firm. While there are more than 200,000 single-establishment firms with sales volumes between $0.5 million and $2 million, there may be an additional 50,000 to 100,000 firms of that size, which at any one time may not be included in the EIS file. The absence of any Census breakdowns by size of firms makes it difficult for us to be more precise. Because of the high degree of corporate concentration in the American economy, however, the absence of even 100,000 firms with average sales of $1 million each would not affect the EIS coverage of total sales value of $3 trillion by more than one-third of 1%.

access to the database

The maintenance of the EIS Database of 360,000 plus records requires deletions, additions, and changes involving over 25,000 records each quarter. It would be clearly uneconomic to "publish" the Database in a permanent printed form only to have it outdated in a few months. Indeed, the great virtue of maintaining information in database form as opposed to publication is the ease with which corrections can be made.

The ideal mode of public access to a computer database is by way of online networks of telephone-linked terminals. The EIS Database has been available in this way since 1975 through worldwide networks as one of about sixty professional databases in the subject areas of Science, Technology, Engineering, Social Sciences, and Business and Economics, mounted by the Lockheed Information Retrieval Service.

Information retrieval software has in the past decade completely altered the way in which librarians and researchers use bibliographic reference sources in database format. The DIALOG retrieval commands developed by the Lockheed Information Retrieval Service enable a user at a remote terminal to find quickly

input/output databases

any group of records in large centralized, periodically updated databases. Hundreds of users can simultaneously obtain access to a given database from points scattered literally over the globe, twenty hours in the day, enjoying the full power of the computer to pinpoint and array records in a variety of ways.

With the DIALOG commands, a user can examine establishments taken from the EIS Database in any combination of states, counties, cities, zip code areas, metropolitan markets, owning companies, 4-digit Standard Industrial Classification (SIC) indus-

table 2–4

applying the lockheed dialog system to eis database*

Marketer's Commands (Questions)	Computer's Responses (Answers)	What Takes Place
1. Select CN = Hamilton, Ohio	1. 676 CN = Ohio, Hamilton	Q. Select all manufacturing plants in Hamilton County (code CN), Ohio. A. There are 676 plants in Hamilton County.
2. Select PC = 2085 Select PC = 2819 Select PC = 2821 Select PC = 2834	2. 87 PC = 2085 3. 422 PC = 2819 4. 373 PC = 2821 5. 430 PC = 2834	Q. Select the plants whose product codes (code PC) are SIC 2085 (distilled and blended liquors), SIC 2819 (industrial inorganic chemicals), SIC 2821 (plastic materials and resins), and SIC 2834 (pharmaceutical preparations). A. There are 87 plants in SIC 2085, 422 plants in SIC 2819, 373 plants in SIC 2821, and 430 plants in SIC 2834.
3. Combine 1 and (2 or 3 or 4 or 5)	6. 14	Q. Create the set of all plants in Hamilton County in the selected industries. A. There are 14 plants that satisfy all the above conditions.

At this point, the computer has arranged the sets of information the marketer wants. In the final two steps, the computer simply ranks the plants in descending order, and prints the plant records.

4. Sort 6/1-14/PC/SD, D	7. 14 6/1-14/PC/SD/, D	Sort all plants by industry (code PC), by shipments volume (code SD) in descending order (code D)
5. Type 7/5/1-14	8. National Distillers Pdts. 120 Section Rd. Cincinnati, Ohio 45216 County: Hamilton 513-948-4000 2085 Liquor Sales $Mil.: 163.2 Industry %: 5.79 Employment: 7(1,000-2,499) National Dstlr. Chem. 99 Park Ave., New York, N.Y. 10016	Type out (format 5) all 14 plants. Printout will include plant's name, street address, city and state, county, phone number, SIC code number, industry name, shipments volume, share of industry shipments, employment size, and name and address of owning company.

*Reprinted from Sales and Marketing Management, June 13, 1977.

tries, and size classes. Table 2–4 illustrates the DIALOG commands and computer responses to queries made by a user wishing to examine plants in a specified county—Hamilton, Ohio; in specified industries—SIC 2085 (Distilled and Blended Liquors), SIC 2819 (Industrial Inorganic Chemicals), SIC 2821 (Plastic Materials and Resins), and SIC 2834 (Pharmaceutical Preparations).

The first command, for example, creates a set consisting of all manufacturing plants in Hamilton County. The second command creates four additional sets, each one made up of all the plants in the United States in SICs 2085, 2819, 2821, and 2834, respectively. The third command combines the five sets into one, yielding a sixth set of only those plants in the four SIC industries located in Hamilton County. The fourth command ranks those plants in descending order of size (determined by shipments dollars) within each SIC. The fifth command instructs the computer to print out the desired plant records on the teletype terminal.

Finally, we should note that there are two additional modes of timesharing access to the EIS file, as provided by TRW and Control Data. Control Data offers a computational service as opposed to the so-called "information retrieval" services of both Lockheed and TRW. Table 2–5 represents a sample TRW Credit Report for a business location, which could be quickly secured by a credit manager seated at a remote terminal anywhere in the United States. The report will show how quickly that business location is paying for purchases made in the most recent time period. Such information comes from a database maintained by the TRW Credit Division, taken from weekly compilations of the credit experience of the nation's 1,000 largest companies, whose combined sales force undoubtedly handle the bulk of the purchases of the American business community. The number of business locations in the TRW database is in the millions, far in excess of the 350,000 locations that will be in the EIS file by the close of 1978.*

Nevertheless, it has been found that a substantial percentage of locations for which credit information is requested can be found in the EIS file. For such locations, which can be found and matched by computer to EIS records despite differences in spelling and nomenclature, the user receives EIS data on total sales, employment, industry, phone number, and parent affiliation, as supplemental data to the credit decision to be made. While credit infor-

---

* According to *County Business Patterns,* the official annual Department of Commerce publication, there are about 350,000 firms covered by Social Security and Unemployment Insurance programs, with twenty or more employees, including farms, banks, and nonprofit industries like health and education. However, *County Business Patterns* does not include, nor will the EIS file attempt to do so, government locations.

table 2–5
nacm business credit experience report

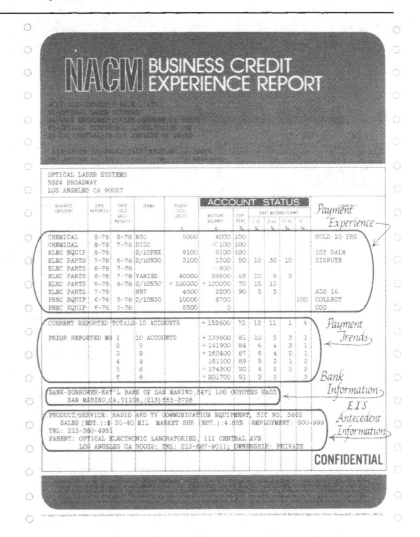

mation is generally thought to be desired for smaller firms, to the extent that the EIS Database accounts for so large a proportion of total purchases, EIS locations tend to have a high probability that they will be targeted for credit requests.

The availability of access to the EIS Database through the timesharing networks of such companies as Lockheed, TRW, and Control Data carries some interesting implications about the role of private agencies in the collection and analysis of business information, as distinct from the role of government in this area. To a limited extent these commercial information services may supply some of the information required by government agencies without adding to the paperwork burden, particularly onerous for small business, that would be entailed by additional governmental mail surveys. And unlike government surveys that must shield the identity of responders, commercial services can "name names."

Thus, the EIS/Lockheed service is now widely used by information specialists in the Department of Commerce to answer questions about specified establishments in specified industries and areas that could not be answered in such detail from Census tabulations. It is also easy to see that the TRW Business Credit Database could someday serve as a periodic barometer of how quickly business is paying its bills. Use of the EIS classification criteria on industry and size of establishment could offer quick readings, in aggregate format, of the current state of business by area, by sector, and by firm. Statisticians from TRW and EIS are now preparing such reports, based on a sample of over 100,000 locations for which statistical summaries can be prepared, on the percentage of outstanding accounts that have gone unpaid for thirty days, sixty days, and more than ninety days, distilled into a single measure of the average number of days required for payment. In this way it will be possible to measure, over time, and by industry, or by company, changes in business liquidity. Indeed had such a service been available in 1970, it would have been possible perhaps for any user to request payments reports for all Penn Central locations, and to have noted a systematic and ominous lengthening of the time required to pay bills well in advance of the final announcement of bankruptcy.

the accuracy of the eis estimate of sales

With the exception of the EIS estimate of a plant's sales volume and its resulting market share, all other elements (name, address, etc.) in the typical EIS record can be traced to such public sources as telephone directories, state and industrial directories, corporate annual reports, and Census Bureau statistics on the size, location, SIC code, and industrial concentration in each industry. Increasing online access to the EIS Database has exposed the EIS sales estimates to heavy public scrutiny. Questions are increasingly raised as to how these estimates are derived, and the level of confidence one can repose in them.

Great care is taken to ensure that a plant's employment level and SIC code conforms with Census Bureau usage, as indicated by published Census control totals available annually for establishments summarized by industries, states, and counties.

The reason for the emphasis on attaining accurate SIC and employment codes is that the EIS establishment Database is designed to interface with an EIS Input/Output Database, which is a matrix, again based primarily on Census Bureau data, tracing the annual deliveries for nearly 1,000 products and services (defined at 4-, 5-, 6-, and 7-digit levels of SIC detail) to 430 manufacturing industries defined at the 4-digit SIC level (see Chapter 3).

In the context of input/output theory, the average relationship of purchases to employment is determined by the technology of the purchasing industry. In the same way, the average relationship between an industry's sales and employment reflects that industry's technology. This becomes obvious from an examination of the variation in these ratios by industry. Thus in capital-intensive industries such as Chemical and Petroleum Products, sales per employee ratios range over $200,000 as against ratios of less than $20,000 in labor-intensive industries such as Apparel and Leather Manufacturing.

The EIS estimate of sales for each establishment is calculated by multiplying the plant employment by the ratio of sales to employment in the industry in which the plant is classified. The underlying assumption is that all establishments in a given industry share a common technology and operate at the average industry-wide level of productivity.

As we shall see, this assumption is generally sufficient to ensure an acceptable order of accuracy for estimating the input requirements of an establishment whose size and SIC code is correctly ascertained. In any case, there are no practicable alternatives to this method of calculating input requirements, since even the accounting procedures followed by most establishments do not allow for keeping annual schedules of purchases, aside from the quinquennial reports to the Census Bureau.

The annual sales of companies, however, are carefully recorded at both the establishment and enterprise level by the companies themselves and by the Census Bureau, at least for large companies. It therefore becomes possible to introduce adjustments into the EIS establishment estimates of shipments when such establishments can be tied to a company whose domestic sales volume is ascertainable. Thus there are two ways in which the EIS sales estimates are adjusted to reflect the fact that the establishment operates at a level of productivity different from that of the industry in which it is classified.

The EIS Database reserves a "shipments" field for a preliminary establishment sales estimate, derived by multiplying the establishment employment by the industry shipments per employee ratio. For companies for which EIS can ascertain an annual domestic sales total, the "sales" field allows for an adjusted estimate of establishment shipments reconciled to a reported total sales figure given for all establishments owned by the company.

This simple but effective procedure enables EIS to take advantage of the continuous flow of articles in the business press about new and growing companies. In this way, for thousands of companies, often small and privately owned, EIS establishment sales estimates will reflect a high degree of currency and accuracy, based on a daily review of the business press.

There is even occasional press coverage on product line breakdowns for large companies operating in many industries. Here EIS relies heavily on the annual publication by the Census Bureau of the "concentration ratios" or percent of sales of the top four, eight, and twenty companies in each 4-digit industry. These ratios are keypunched when published, and a special computer program compares them with corresponding Database ratios in order to focus attention on significant divergences.

While the Census Bureau cannot reveal the identities of the large companies, an attempt to compare such percentages with those derived from the EIS Database invariably will draw attention to the reasons for major divergences and the consequent need for adjustment for large companies.

For example, the Census Bureau reported that in 1972 the top four companies accounted for 54% of total sales of SIC 3573 (Computers and Computing Equipment), a figure that was far higher than the preliminary EIS estimate for the top four companies, which included IBM as the largest single company. This suggested that the initial EIS estimates of shipments of IBM computer plants, based on plant employment, were systematically too low. It was found that the true magnitude of the sales value of the computers shipped from IBM plants rests not only on the level of employment at the producing plants, but also on almost an equal number of employees engaged elsewhere in service and maintenance, design, programming, etc., all of which increases the ratio of sales to the number of IBM production workers to a degree not reflected in the average establishment relationships reported for other companies.

Over the years, these various types of "company" sales adjustments, often supplemented by informed guesses by competitors, have resulted in the storage in the EIS sales field of thousands of "product line" sales estimates for large companies even when they operate in many markets.

We are now in a position to address the question: How "accurate" is an EIS estimate of sales or purchase for any single establishment or plant? Three main sources of error must be considered: whether the "correct" SIC code has been assigned to the plant; whether the average annual employment level of the plant has been correctly ascertained; and finally whether we have correctly allowed for variations in plant productivity or efficiency of materials consumed per employee from the assumed industry-wide "technical coefficient,"* not accounted for by company adjustments of the kind described above.

The pattern of variation in productivity ratios within industries is revealed by data from the Census of Manufactures on the relationship between shipments and employment within various size classes in each 4-digit industry.

In most industries the highest levels of productivity or efficiency in the use of materials per employee are achieved in the middle-size levels and fall off somewhat in both very small and very large plants. Thus, according to Census of Manufactures data, three-quarters of all (4-digit) industries reported highest levels of productivity in plants falling into the middle-size range.

Very small plants evidently do not enjoy the economies of scale available to larger plants, whereas very large plants may also discharge central administrative functions and therefore include employees who do not contribute directly to plant-production efficiency. Nevertheless the divergence in productivity among all size classes is generally less than 25% or 30%. Indeed, divergences of higher magnitude would affect the ability of relatively less efficient plants to compete at all with other plants in that industry.

One key factor to keep in mind is that the degree of accuracy of EIS sales data for each establishment in a multiplant company can be calculated only if the true sales figure of each establishment is known. Such knowledge is rarely publicly available; and even in unpublished corporate accounting records where establishment sales figures may be recorded, the accounting techniques that generate sales totals for each establishment are subject to at least as much error as the input/output techniques used by EIS for estimating sales in each plant.

For instance, integrated industrial complexes, such as steel mills, petrochemical plants, and paper mills, will often show a different sales mix in corporate annual reports than the actual shipments of the plants comprising the complex. The accounting procedures of a tissue producer might assign all revenues to the sale of tissue while incorporating the value of pulp and paper in the tissue. The Census Bureau would, in contrast, show the value of shipments of the pulp, paper, and tissue as nonadditive totals.

---

*There are, of course, other assumptions that can be made to account for divergence from the "truth"; for example, that all employees in the plant are engaged in the indicated primary activity, thus ignoring variations in productivity associated with secondary activities.

summary of eis procedures

The entire universe of plants employing twenty or more (accounting for 95% of industrial activity) is compiled from public records of all types. Of these establishments, perhaps 2% are dead, 1% is missing, and 2% represent duplicate locations, or locations with erroneous names, addresses, employment, etc.

Sales of each establishment are calculated on the basis of the average shipments per employee for each industry (as reported by the Census Bureau), and the sales of all establishments are then summarized by parent companies, where the sum of the sales is reconciled with data in the corporate annual reports.

This last step minimizes the source of error that can arise when companies have an atypical product mix or atypical employee productivity levels because some corresponding allowance will be reflected in the total sales of the company.

Thus, the speculation that EIS sales estimates per establishment vary by as much as 25% for the actual sales of each establishment is, in some respects, fruitless because there is no certain way to measure this divergence. Nevertheless, conceding a 25% standard error of estimate for any given observation, the impact can be measured as follows:

On the establishment level, an EIS estimate of sales of $1,000,000 would mean that there is a 67% probability that the true sales figure for the establishment lies between $750,000 and $1,250,000.*

The EIS Database greatly facilitates the choice of samples large enough to meet any desired level of accuracy, particularly in association with the facts on industrial concentration. Knowing that about 80% of total sales or purchases will generally be accounted for by the top 20% of all records, we can, if we like, sort any group of 10,000 records in high-to-low sequence and base our analysis on merely the top 2,000 records with only a 20% loss of coverage.

DIALOG users of the EIS Database will find it cumbersome (but possible) to add manually the sales estimates of large groups of EIS records, if they wish to calculate confidence limits for any

---

* No estimate of accuracy could be based on a single estimate; the relevant criterion of accuracy for any group of n EIS records would be indicated by the formula for the standard error of the mean, $\sqrt{\sigma/n}$. Thus, for any 100 independently selected EIS records, the standard error of the mean or sum of the sales or purchases of these plants would be $\sqrt{.25/100} = .05$. This means there is a 67% probability that the true sum or mean lies within ±5% of the indicated sum or mean of the 100 observations. A ten-fold increase in accuracy, however, can be achieved by a one hundred-fold increase in the size of the sample. Thus, if the standard error for any single observation was 25%, the standard error of the sum of 10,000 observations would be $\sqrt{.25/10000} = .005$. We can then attach a 95% degree of confidence to the statement that the indicated sum of 10,000 observations lies within three standard errors, or 1.5% of the "truth."

group.* But for most market research problems, relatively small samples will yield meaningful results, particularly if the analyst can stratify the sample in terms of the desired criteria or constraints.

We are now in a position to appreciate the enormous power of Lockheed's DIALOG information retrieval system as applied to the EIS Database. A Lockheed user can issue commands at a terminal that will, within a matter of minutes, select, sort, and print any desired number of records, based on any desired combination of constraints on area, size, industry, or company ownership. It is a truly staggering fact that the user can select a group literally from trillions of possibilities!

It is instructive to see how such a calculation can be made. Here, for example, are all the ways in which geographic and other constraints can be imposed on the selection of records from the EIS file:

the number of possible eis group selections

A. Geographic Fields	
10 Regions	$(10)^1$
50 States	$5(10)^1$
3,000 Counties	$3(10)^3$
10,000 Cities	$(10)^4$
30,000 5-Digit Zip Code Areas	$3(10)^4$
10,000 4-Digit Zip Code Areas	$(10)^4$
800 3-Digit Zip Code Areas	$8(10)^2$
B. Other Searchable Fields	
430 4-Digit SIC Codes	$4.3(10)^2$
140 3-Digit SIC Codes	$1.4(10)^2$
20 2-Digit SIC Codes	$2(10)^1$
50,000 Companies	$5(10)^4$
1000 Fortune Companies	$(10)^3$
Total	$(216)(10)^{33}$

Since each of the possible groups to be selected can be combined with any other group, the total number of different group combinations is the astronomical figure of $(216)(10)^{33}$. And since there are six different possible ways to use the three COMBINE commands (OR, AND, NOT) the theoretical universe of unique final EIS groups is about $(13)(10)^{36}$, or 13 trillion trillion trillion.

Other Lockheed users may come up with alternative estimates of this universe, but the point should now be clear—we are deal-

---

* Lockheed has added a computational facility to the Predicasts Statistical Files, and expects to be able to do this eventually for EIS too. Computational programs for realtime access to the EIS files are also available from the Cybernetics Division of Control Data Corporation.

ing with an awesome facility that, when properly used, should represent a challenge to the research community to devise new questions that could not have been previously posed or answered.

Since the EIS Manufacturing Database has only 120,000 records, perhaps most of the trillions of possible combinations represent empty cells, i.e., no-hits. Thus, no user should realistically select a group using several constraints in a single command without some expectation of securing a hit. It should be evident from the above exercise that the DIALOG access to the EIS file performs best for "needle-in-the-haystack" types of problems, in which the speed and power of DIALOG's ability to search and compare many groups of records will yield a comparatively small number of hits. Thus, it would be wasteful to use this facility to secure massive lists for purposes of mailing or prospect identification insofar as there are more cost-efficient methods of generating or purchasing directory-type lists for use in mailing, customer prospecting, etc. If, however, one wanted the list confined to certain industries and/or sizes, there would not be any published equivalent available.

As a final note, for the user who wishes to upgrade the accuracy of any group of selected EIS records, there is an important correctional component embodied in each record: its telephone number. More often than not, a phone call will resolve all doubts about the informational content of the record. Feedback from EIS users who have made such calls has now become an important component of EIS maintenance procedures.

chapter 3

input/output databases and technology

An input/output matrix represents a giant storehouse of technological information on the input requirements of each industry arrayed as columns in an input/output table (see Table 3–15). Reading down any one column, the direct transactions figures appearing in each cell record the purchases of the buying industry from each of the selling industries represented as rows. These direct transactions or purchases, when expressed as dollars of input required to produce a unit of output, are called "technical coefficients."

technical coefficients

In the quinquennial input/output tables prepared by the Bureau of Economic Analysis (BEA) of the U.S. Department of Commerce, direct transactions or "technical coefficients" are available for a matrix of nearly 400 industries defined at 3- and 4-digit levels of

---

* A brief note about the analytical significance of the Standard Industrial Classification System is in order. Developed by the U.S. Census Bureau over the past seven decades, the SIC system has become a model now followed by most of the central statistical offices of the nations of the world. The system defines both industries and product classes so that the scope of the category becomes progressively narrower with successive addition of numerical digits, as in the following example:

Standard Industrial Classification Code	Designation	Name
20	Major Industry Group	Food and Kindred Products
201	Industry Group	Meat Products
2011	Industry	Meat Packing Plants
20111	Product Class	Fresh Beef
etc.		

the Standard Industrial Classification (SIC) System.* While many of the 160,000 possible cells are blank because all industries do not sell directly to all other industries, it is easy to appreciate that such an input/output table can be viewed, at the very least, as an enormously efficient way to summarize thousands of markets in which the buying-selling transactions of hundreds of industries take place.

As economists well know, it is the special virtue of input/output analysis that knowledge of the "direct coefficients" can, with the advent of the computer, also yield mathematical solutions to determine the "indirect coefficients" that link industries together. These indirect coefficients make it possible to trace both the direct and indirect impact on all industries that could arise from a change in any one input or output cell.

EIS maintains a matrix, derived in large part from the same Census information on which the BEA tables are based, that traces the annual direct deliveries for nearly 1,000 products and services (defined at 4-, 5-, 6-, and 7-digit levels of detail) to each of about 700 possible purchasing industries, defined at the 4-digit SIC level. This can be visualized as a rectangular matrix with 700,000 (1,000 × 700) possible transactions.*

The programs providing the computational interface between this rectangular input/output database and the EIS Database of Business Enterprise discussed in Chapter 2 are based on the assumption that all establishments classified in a given 4-digit SIC share a common technology. For some industry classifications, this assumption requires considerable qualification, but it permits us to allocate industry purchases for the 1,000 items among all the establishments classified in each 4-digit industry, with a consequent enormous expansion of the informational content of the input/output matrix. The allocations among all establishments within a single industry are made on the basis of the size of each establishment.

analysis of current industrial demands

The resultant "information explosion" can be illustrated with a series of reports detailing the purchasing patterns for corrugated shipping boxes.

Corrugated boxes represent a basic packaging material required in about 300 manufacturing industries defined at the 4-digit level. In 1975, for example, these industries, employing some 15 million persons, purchased 200 billion square feet of corrugated

---

* See Appendix B, Selector List, p. 116, for a listing, in SIC sequence, of many of these products and services.

boxes valued at $4.4 billion, representing an average requirement per employee of 13 thousand square feet valued at about $300.

The packaging requirements of each industry vary widely with respect to the bulk, value, perishability, etc., of the product shipped, as would be revealed by an examination of a row of "technical coefficients" for corrugated boxes, as displayed in an input/output table (see Table 3–15). In industries like glass containers, for example, where the output is so susceptible to shipping damage, the box requirement per employee is as high as 240 thousand square feet valued at close to $5,000.

In fact, corrugated boxes represent the largest input in the "recipe" for making glass containers, as would be revealed by an examination of all the technical coefficients in the input/output column headed by "glass containers." Corrugated boxes are so crucial to the production of glass containers that some glass container companies, like Owens-Illinois, manufacture their own corrugated boxes.

In a similar way the packaging requirements for each industry would be determined by a mix of technological, marketing, and price considerations that in any given year make the technical coefficient a "state of the art" indicator within that industry.

In expanding the input/output matrix from the industry to the establishment level, the assumption of common technology within a single industry in effect requires us to calculate that every glass container plant will require corrugated boxes at the rate of $5,000 or 240 thousand square feet per employee. That this is an oversimplification is evident from statistics available from the Census of Manufactures on the relationship between employment and total cost of materials within various size classes in each 4-digit industry.

A fairly consistent pattern emerges from these figures: in most industries the highest levels of productivity or efficiency in the use of materials per employee are achieved in the middle-size levels, and fall off somewhat in both very small and very large plants. Thus according to Census of Manufactures data, three-quarters of all (4-digit) industries reported highest levels of productivity in plants falling into the middle-size range.*

As noted in Chapter 2, small plants do not enjoy the economies of scale available to larger plants while, on the other hand, very large plants may include central administrative employees who do not contribute directly to plant-production efficiency. This accounts for some degree of systematic divergence in productivity among

---

*Cf. John M. Blair, *Economic Concentration: Structure, Behavior and Public Policy,* (New York: Harcourt Brace Jovanovich, 1972), p. 98.

all size classes, but the range is generally less than 25% or 30%, else the ability of relatively less efficient plants to compete at all with other plants in that industry would be affected.

The practical consequences of this application of the assumption of common technology in the case of corrugated boxes should be examined.

The computer programs that produced Tables 3–1 to 3–8 in effect first estimate the potential consumption of corrugated boxes of each of some 90,000 plants in the 300 odd industries that require corrugated boxes as a packaging material, and then go on to rearrange and print out the information by area, industry, and company ownership in a variety of formats.

A report listing the available information on each of the 90,000 plants would require 1,800 pages (with 50 plants to a page). If complete listings were provided for all the different formats and sequences available (alphabetically, high to low, national accounts, geographically by state, county, zip code, telephone area code, etc.), we would need a 12-foot shelf to contain them all.

Such a mass of data would be difficult to digest by any one person. Fortunately, the computer can be used for condensation and summarization, so that the key facts about the industrial consumption patterns for this product (and all other products) can be contained on a few summary pages of the following reports:

National Market Size Report (Table 3–1)
This is the key Database report summarizing potential purchases (or consumption) in each industry at both the 4-digit and 2-digit level of SIC detail. A statistical summary of the employment size structure is provided for each buying industry, as well as the ratio of purchases-per-employee, which is the "technical coefficient" responsible for allocating industry purchases to all plants in a given industry. Such information would be of interest for corporate planning and high-level sales management functions.

State Market Size Report (Table 3–2)
This report provides a statistical summary of consumption by industry in each state, of interest to regional sales managers.

County Market Size Report (Table 3–3)
This report summarizes consumption by industry at the county level within states, of interest to regional or district sales managers.

Establishment Buying Power Report (Table 3–4)
This report provides the plant detail underlying the preceding county summary report, of interest to the salesman assigned to the area.

table 3-1
national market size report
(case study: corrugated shipping containers)

SIC	DESCRIPTION	NUMBER OF PLANTS WITH EMPLOYMENT OF						ESTIMATED CONSUMPTION	TOTAL EMPLOY	RATIO PER EMPLOYEE
		20-49	50-99	100-249	250-499	500-OVER	TOTAL			
2834	PHARMACEUTICAL PREPARATIONS	139	99	106	49	64	457	880,802	134,523	6.55
2841	SOAP AND OTHER DETERGENTS	103	43	33	10	15	204	1,991,897	30,788	64.70
2842	POLISHES AND SANITATION GOODS	235	112	75	18	11	451	802,392	40,111	20.00
2843	SURFACE ACTIVE AGENTS	23	16	10		2	51	249,247	4,439	56.15
2844	PERFUMES & OTHER TOILET PREP	46	47	52	31	33	209	2,312,672	56,022	41.28
2851	PAINTS AND ALLIED PRODUCTS	415	143	132	41	14	745	1,234,978	64,925	19.04
2861	GUM AND WOOD CHEMICALS	33	22	25	1	3	84	106,320	8,876	11.98

SIC	DESCRIPTION	NUMBER OF PLANTS WITH EMPLOYMENT						ESTIMATED CONSUMPTION	TOTAL EMPLOYMENT
		20-49	50-99	100-249	250-499	500-OVER	TOTAL		
26	PAPER AND ALLIED PRODUCTS	939	725	775	320	241	3000	21,218,689	535,617
27	PRINTING AND PUBLISHING	2715	1672	854	316	172	5729	3,090,139	586,626
28	CHEMICALS AND ALLIED PRODUCTS	2144	1170	967	405	390	5076	14,832,514	871,495
29	PETROLEUM AND COAL PRODUCTS	253	167	161	77	51	709	1,648,015	134,747
30	RUBBER AND PLASTICS PRODUCTS	1418	975	954	343	230	3920	9,270,290	605,024
	US TOTALS	36486	23480	20547	8856	5796	95165	196,490,379	15,093,969

Description: This format identifies the industries that buy your product. It tells you how big your total market is; how much of the market each industry accounts for; how many prospective customer establishments there are in each industry; and how many are large, medium and small establishments. It also shows you the consumption-per-employee ratio used to allocate the quantities bought by each industry to the individual establishments in the industry.

Use: This format gives you the information you need to proportion your marketing effort to the actual buying power of your various industry prospects; and to focus on large establishments in industries where consumption-per-employee is low, and smaller ones where consumption-per-employee is high.

Note: SIC 2844 (The Perfumes, Cosmetics and Toilet Preparations Industry) purchases 2,312,672 MSF (thousand square feet) of Corrugated Shipping Containers per year. This industry comprises 209 establishments, of which 33 have over 500 employees.

table 3-2
state market size report
(case study: corrugated shipping containers)

| | NUMBER OF ESTABLISHMENTS WITH EMPLOYMENT OF | | | | | | |
	20-49	50-99	200-249	250-499	500-OVER	TOTAL	CONSUMPTION
STATE OF NEW JERSEY							
2824 NONCELLULOSIC ORGANIC FIBERS	2					2	494
2831 BIOLOGICAL PRODUCTS	2		3			5	4,871
2833 MEDICINALS AND BOTANICALS	4	6	4	2	3	19	24,371
2834 PHARMACEUTICAL PREPARATIONS	14	6	23	9	10	62	171,670
2841 SOAP AND OTHER DETERGENTS	5	7	5	1	1	19	163,693
2842 POLISHES AND SANITATION GOODS	19	9	9	3	1	41	83,080
2843 SURFACE ACTIVE AGENTS	4	2			1	7	61,541
2844 PERFUMES & OTHER TOILET PREP	4	8	8	8	12	40	760,460
2851 PAINTS AND ALLIED PRODUCTS	54	13	10	5	1	83	114,297
STATE TOTALS	2,757	1,459	1,021	346	229	5,812	12,190,578

Description: This format breaks down the market for your product according to state. It tells you how big your market is in each state; which customer industries operate in each state; how much of your product each industry consumes; and how many establishments there are in each customer industry.

Use: With this format, you can determine which customer industries are predominant in each state, and insure that salesmen specializing in those industries are assigned to the state in sufficient strength. You can use the data on overall market size (and number of prospects) in each state as a basis for setting sales quotas, and for analyzing requirements for establishing nearby production and/or distribution facilities.

Note: In the State of New Jersey, there are 40 prospective customer establishments in SIC 2844 (Perfumes, Cosmetics and Toilet Preparations). These establishments buy 760,460 MSF of Corrugated Shipping Containers.

table 3-3
county market size report
(case study: corrugated shipping containers)

2653 CORRUGATED SHIPPING CONT	NUMBER OF ESTABLISHMENTS WITH EMPLOYMENT OF					TOTAL	CONSUMPTION
	20-49	50-99	100-249	250-499	500-OVER		
NEW JERSEY							
BERGEN 003							
2841 SOAP AND OTHER DETERGENTS	1	2	1		1	5	79,905
2842 POLISHES AND SANITATION GOODS	4	5	2			11	16,000
2844 PERFUMES & OTHER TOILET PREP	2	1	2	4	2	11	135,770
2851 PAINTS AND ALLIED PRODUCTS	13	4	1	1		19	23,933
2865 CYCLIC INTERMEDIATES AND CRUDES	4	2	1	3		10	9,027
COUNTY TOTALS	550	244	176	64	29	1,063	1,898,205
WARREN 041							
3648 LIGHTING EQUIP, NEC			1			1	550
3677 ELECTRONIC COILS, TRANSFORMERS			1			1	222
3949 SPORTING AND ATHLETIC GOODS		1				1	358
COUNTY TOTALS	14	16	11	5	4	50	134,460
STATE TOTALS	2,757	1,459	1,021	346	229	5,812	12,190,578

Description: This format tells you how big your market is in each county; which customer industries operate in each county; how much of your product each of those industries consumes; and how many establishments there are in each customer industry.

Use: This format is most valuable as a marketing or corporate planning tool. It enables you to assemble contiguous counties into sales territories of desired geographic size—and then allocate your selling resources to those territories in proportion to their actual buying potential, and the number of buying units they contain. You can also use the data as a basis for setting up sales territories of approximately equal market potential.

Note: In Bergen County, in New Jersey, there are 11 prospective customer establishments in SIC 2844 (Perfumes, Cosmetics and Toilet Preparations). These establishments buy 135,770 MSF of Corrugated Shipping Containers, or approximately 1% of the total consumption in New Jersey.

table 3-4
establishment buying power report
(case study: corrugated shipping containers)

NEW JERSEY

BERGEN   003

SIC	NAME OF ESTABLISHMENT	ADDRESS	CITY	ZIP	PHONE	CONSUMPTION	EMPL
2842	RUSTAIN PRODUCTS	545 MIDLAND AVE	SADDLE BROOK	07662	201-796 1181	400	20
2844	LANMAN & KEMP BARCLAY	15 GRAND AVE	PALISADES PK	07650	201-943 3100	1,444	35
2844	LEHN & FINK DV STERLING	225 SUMMIT AV	MONTVALE	07645	201-391 8500	33,024	800
2844	LOFT-TANGEE INC	65 RAILROAD AVE	RIDGEFIELD	07657	201-945 5800	24,768	600
2844	LOFT TANGEE INC	400 GOTHAM PKWY	CARLSTADT	07072	201-935 1700	4,128	100
2844	MEM CO INC	UNION ST EXTN	NORTHVALE	07647	201-767 0100	12,384	300
2844	PRIVTE LABL CSMTC CO INC	20 10 MAPLE AVE	FAIR LAWN	07410	201-423 1515	9,081	220
2844	ROURE BERTRAND DUPONT	1775 WINDSOR RD	TEANECK	07666	201-832 2300	1,609	39
3999	SCHOLL MANUFACTURING CO	235 MURRAY HILL PKWY	E RUTHERFORD	07073	201-933 0600	143	40
3999	SILK-O-LITE LAMPSHADES	100 OUTWATER LANE	GARFIELD	07026	201-478 7212	359	100
3999	SMITH & NICHOLS INC	620 CENTRAL AVE	CARLSTADT	07072	201-438 3194	107	30
				COUNTY TOTAL		1,898,205	

Description: This format identifies the individual establishments that consume your product. It furnishes name, address, phone number and nature of business for each establishment. It groups them by industry within each state and each county, and estimates how much of your product each establishment buys.

Use: This format can be considered the salesman's daily prospect book. It encourages sales prospecting, because it pinpoints the establishments which have the greatest probability of being major customers. It organizes the listings in a convenient geographic arrangement to help a salesman plan his itineraries most efficiently.

Note: Loft-Tangee, Inc., at 65 Railroad Avenue in Ridgefield, has 600 employees and buys approximately 24,768 MSF of Corrugated Shipping Containers.

table 3–5
key account report, by state
(case study: corrugated shipping containers)

RANK	SIC	NAME OF ESTABLISHMENT	ADDRESS	CITY	ST	ZIP	PHONE	EMPL	CONSUMPTION
56	2844	MENNEN CO INC	HANOVER AVE	MORRISTOWN	NJ	07960	201-538 7100	750	30,960
57	3411	CONTINENTAL CAN CO	297 GETTY AVE	PATERSON	NJ	07501	201-525 4800	900	30,726
58	3429	TERNSTEDT DIV GMC	PARKWAY AVE	TRENTON	NJ	08628	609-882 1000	3400	29,648
59	2032	VENICE MAID CO INC	NORTH MILL RD	VINELAND	NJ	08360	609-691 2100	350	28,150
60	2654	CREST CONT CORP	MILLVILLE IND PK	MILLVILLE	NJ	08020	609-825 1450	225	27,751
61	2641	ARVEY CORP	300 COMMUNIPAW AV	JERSEY CITY	NJ	07304	201-333 5000	300	26,676
62	2035	CPC INTL/BEST FOODS	99 AVENUE A	BAYONNE	NJ	07002	201-339 6800	500	26,640
63	3497	CELLO VERTO CO LTD	54 60 SECOND AVE	KEARNY	NJ	07032	201-991 7262	50	26,292
64	2013	DEVRO INC DV J & J	SOUTHSIDE AVE	SOMERVILLE	NJ	08876	201-524 0400	306	25,502
65	3253	WENCZEL TILE CO INC	KLAG AVE	TRENTON	NJ	08638	609-599 4503	218	25,346
66	2079	STANDARD BRANDS	8030 NATIONAL HWY	PENNSAUKEN	NJ	08110	609-665 1650	150	25,113
67	2013	SABRETT FOOD PROD	50 COLDEN	JERSEY CITY	NJ	07302	201-434 7062	300	25,002
68	2844	BLOCK DRUG CO INC	257 CORNELISON AV	JERSEY CITY	NJ	07302	201-434 3000	600	24,768
69	2844	LOFT-TANGEE INC	65 RAILROAD AVE	RIDGEFIELD	NJ	07657	201-945 5800	600	24,768
70	2654	DAIRY PAK	155 E-HANOVER AVE	MORRISTOWN	NJ	07960	201-539 5600	200	24,668
71	2099	COCA COLA/TENCO DV	720 EDGAR RD	LINDEN	NJ	07036	201-862 6600	466	24,404

Description: This format ranks your prospective customer establishments in each state, in order of their importance as buyers. (It can also be structured along the lines of your sales territories.) It shows you the amount of product used by each prospect.

Use: This format is especially useful for concentrating sales effort on the cream of the market, since it enables you to single out, at a glance, the top group of buying establishments in each state (or territory). It is equally valuable as a marketing tool, because it tells you how many prospects must be converted to achieve any given share of market; who those prospects are; and how much each of them buys.

Note: Loft-Tangee, Inc. at 65 Railroad Avenue ranks 69th in the State of New Jersey in consumption of Corrugated Shipping Containers.

41

table 3-6
key account report, nationwide
(case study: corrugated shipping containers)

RANK	SIC	ESTABLISHMENT	ADDRESS	CITY	ST	ZIP	PHONE	EMPL	CONSUMPTION	PCT CUM
1,101	2844	ANDREW JERGENS CO	2535 SPRING GROVE	CINCINNATI	OH	45214	513-521 1400	600	24,768	35.25
1,102	2844	BLOCK DRUG CO INC	257 CORNELISON AV	JERSEY CITY	NJ	07302	201-434 3000	600	24,768	35.26
1,103	2844	KOLMAR LABS	SKYLINE DR BOX 11	PORT JERVIS	NY	12771	914-856 5311	600	24,768	35.27
1,104	2844	LOFT-TANGEE INC	65 RAILROAD AVE	RIDGEFIELD	NJ	07657	201-945 5800	600	24,768	35.28
1,105	2844	TRAVENOL LABS	6301 N LINCOLN	MORTON GROVE	IL	60053	312-965 4700	600	25,768	35.30
1,106	3231	CORNING GLASS WKS	MAIN ST	BIG FLATS	NY	14814	607-974 9000	600	24,068	35.31
1,107	3231	SHATTERPROOF GLASS	4815 CABOT	DETROIT	MI	48210	313-582 6200	600	24,708	35.32
1,108	2654	DAIRY PAK	155 E-HANOVER AVE	MORRISTOWN	NJ	07960	201-539 5600	200	24,668	35.33
1,109	2654	MARYLAND CUP CORP	215 E 7 ST	LOS ANGELES	CA	90023	213-268 3553	200	24,668	35.35
1,110	2654	SMITH LEE CO INC	537 FITCH	ONEIDA	NY	13421	315-363 2500	200	24,668	35.36
95,151	2873	SWIFT AGRI CHEM	1919 SWIFT DR	OAK BROOK	IL	60521	312-325 9320	20	7	99.75
95,152	2873	TYLER FERTILIZER	420 SOUTH OAKLAND	TYLER	TX	75701	214-597 7296	20	7	99.75
							U.S. TOTAL		196,490,379	

Description: This format describes the concentration of buying power for your product on a national basis. It ranks all buying establishments in order of importance, and describes each by name, address, phone, type of business and employment level. It estimates how much of your product each establishment consumes, and traces the cumulative percentage of consumption.

Use: You can use this format as a guide in the selection of key prospects, on a national basis, for sales concentration. In many companies, these prospects are handled by headquarters sales management, rather than by the field sales force, in some cases with local monitoring by regional sales managers.

Note: On a national basis, Loft-Tangee, Inc. at 65 Railroad Avenue in Ridgefield, New Jersey, ranks 1,104th as a consumer of Corrugated Shipping Containers. The top 1,110 locations out of the universe of 95,152 consuming locations account for 35.36% of Corrugated Shipping Containers consumption.

table 3-7
national accounts report
(case study: corrugated shipping containers)

ESTAB/COMPANY NAME	ADDRESS	CITY	ST	ZIP	PHONE	EMPL	SIC	CONSUMPTION
FAB INDUSTRIES INC	200 MADISON AVE	NEW YORK	NY	10016		06622		
FAB LACE INC	200 MADISON AVE	NEW YORK	NY	10016	212-279 9000	30	2221	190
								190
MOHICAN MILLS/FAB IND	WEST FINGER ST	MAIDEN	NC	28650	704-428 9138	175	2256	1,065
MOHICAN MILLS/FAB IND	200 MADISON AVE	LINCOLNTON	NC	28092	704-735 2573	500	2256	3,045
								4,110
				COMPANY TOTALS		705		4,300

PCT OF TOTAL MARKET POTENTIAL =   .00

ESTAB/COMPANY NAME	ADDRESS	CITY	ST	ZIP	PHONE	EMPL	SIC	CONSUMPTION
FABERGE INC	1345 AVE AMERICA	NEW YORK	NY	10019		04187		
FABERGE INC	1750 S TOWNE AVE	POMONA	CA	91766	714-627 1586	185	2844	7,636
RAYETTE FABERGE INC	185 LAFOND ST	ST PAUL	MN	55103	612-224 5651	180	2844	7,430
LOFT-TANGEE INC	65 RAILROAD AVE.	RIDGEFIELD	NJ	07657	201-945 5800	600	2844	24,732
FABERGE INC RAYETTE DV	20 LINDEN AVE E	JERSEY CITY	NJ	07305	201-432 7100	260	2844	10,732
								50,566
TIP TOP PRODUCTS CO INC	1520 CUMING	OMAHA	NB	68102	402-348 9150	600	3964	33,396
								33,396
				COMPANY TOTALS		1825		83,962

PCT OF TOTAL MARKET POTENTIAL =   .04

Description: This format identifies all the companies that are potentially national account prospects. It estimates how much of your product each of these companies buys; it identifies all the establishments owned by each company that buy your product; and it estimates the buying potential of each of those establishments.

Use: This format can serve as the key information base for organizing a national accounts sales program. Where a company is a user of your product, this format will reveal all the establishments owned by that company that use the product, even if they are "hidden" under unrelated and unfamiliar names. This format is insurance against omission of importance prospective customers in the construction of a national accounts program.

Note: Loft-Tangee, Inc., at 65 Railroad Avenue in Ridgefield, New Jersey, is owned by Faberge, Inc. The five Faberge establishments consume approximately 83,962 MSF of Corrugated Shipping Containers, or 0.4% of the U.S. total.

table 3–8
national accounts summary report
(case study: corrugated shipping containers)

COMP CODE	COMPANY/ESTAB NAME	ADDRESS	CITY	ST	ZIP	CONSUMPTION	CUMUL PERCENT	NO. PLTS	RANK
06859	KROGER CO	1014 VINE ST	CINCINNATI	OH	45201	86,845	50.53	19	308
00272	RICELAND FOODS INC	FLOYD ST	JONESBORO	AR	72401	86,409	50.57	3	309
05494	GEORGE D WESTON LTD	3501 COMMERCE COURT W	TORONTO ONT	AK	M5L1C	86,191	50.61	4	310
01425	DRESSER INDUSTRIES	3000 REPUBLIC NATL BNK	DALLAS	TX	75221	85,886	50.65	50	311
02424	ICI UNITED STATES	NEW MURPHY RD/CONCORD PK	WILMINGTON	DE	19899	85,883	50.69	14	312
03705	JENOS INC	525 LAKE AVE S	DULUTH	MN	55801	85,776	50.73	1	313
00885	CHELSEA INDUSTRIES	1369 SOLDIERS FIELD RD	BOSTON	MA	02135	85,455	50.77	22	314
03561	DANTE INC	40 MAYNARD ST	ATTLEBORO	MA	02703	85,284	50.81	1	315
02862	LENOX INC	PRINCE & MEADE STS	TRENTON	NJ	08605	85,011	50.85	15	316
06475	IDEAL TOY CORP	184 10 JAMAICA AVE	HOLLIS	NY	11423	85,009	50.89	3	317
04813	STERLING DRUG INC	90 PARK AVE	NEW YORK	NY	10016	84,652	50.93	19	318
01832	FRUEHAUF CORP	10900 HARPER AVE	DETROIT	MI	48232	84,368	50.97	28	319
04546	SIMMONS CO	280 PARK AVE	NEW YORK	NY	10017	84,308	51.01	20	320
04187	FABERGE INC	1345 AVE AMERICA	NEW YORK	NY	10019	83,962	51.05	5	321
09100	BASF CORP	43-30 CHESAPEAKE DR	CHARLOTTE	NC	28208	83,311	51.09	16	322
03972	STAR CITY GLASS CO	RT 117	COVENTRY	RI	02816	83,174	51.13	1	323
00966	GOULD INC	10 GOULD CENTER	ROLLING MDWS	IL	60008	83,072	51.17	47	324

Description: This format describes the most intense concentration of buying power that can possibly be identified. It summarizes the "parent-child" format (shown on the previous page). It identifies by name and address each parent company that buys your product; specifies the number of establishments owned by each company; and estimates their combined buying power. The companies are ranked in descending order of buying potential.

Use: This format is a valuable tool for analysis of each of your major accounts or prospects. You can readily identify major users by their position at the head of the listing. You can then compare your own sales records to the listing of establishments owned by each major user, and determine if you are reaching all the establishment users of your product in each company.

Note: Faberge, Inc. ranks 321st nationally in consumption of Corrugated Shipping Containers. The top 320 companies consuming Corrugated Shipping Containers account for 50% of all U.S. consumption.

Key Account Report, by State and Nationwide (Tables 3–5 and 3–6)

These reports are high-to-low rankings, available for any geographic area, designed to focus attention on plant concentration patterns, i.e., the relatively small number of plants accounting for the bulk of potential purchases. These reports should be of interest to all levels of management.

National Accounts Report and Summary Report (Tables 3–7 and 3–8)

Concentration of purchasing patterns is about five times greater at the parent company level than at the plant level. Generally speaking, the top 1,000 companies will account for more than three-quarters of total purchases of any given product—the equivalent roughly to the purchases of the top 4,000 or 5,000 establishments. These reports illustrate two formats in which the purchases of companies can be analyzed on a national account basis. They are designed for top management scrutiny, for they offer insights to the most productive kind of salesmanship.

projection of industrial demand

The eight reports discussed above provide enough information about the *current* purchasing patterns for any one product that any manufacturer of that product would want to know. Similar reports can also be prepared to provide *future* projections, as in the case of Tables 3–9, 3–10, and 3–11.

Growth Trends of Customer Industries (Table 3–9)

This table is based on the National Market Size Report (Table 3–1). Here the current shipments of each buying industry is projected to future years by assuming that each industry will continue to increase at the same average annual rate of growth registered over the past Census benchmark interval. (More sophisticated kinds of projection assumptions are also possible.)

Growth Trends of Product Demand in Customer Industries (Table 3–10)

In this report the growth in shipments of each industry is converted into corrugated box demand on the basis of varying assumptions on the relationship between shipments (output) and box demand (input). Depending on the assumed relationship, the latter can be a constant or can vary with each industry.

table 3-9

growth trends of customer industries
(sample printout: corrugated shipping containers—sic 2653)

CUSTOMER INDUSTRY		VALUE OF SHIPMENTS IN CONSTANT DOLLARS ($ MILLIONS)						
		ACTUAL			PROJECTED		ANNUAL GROWTH RATE	
SIC	DESCRIPTION	1967	1972	1975	1980	1985	67-72	72-75
2032	CANNED SPECIALTIES	1,361	1,680	1,905	2,351	2,900	4.29	4.30
2033	CANNED FRUITS, VEGETABLES & JAMS	3,467	3,498	3,516	3,546	3,576	.17	.19
2034	DEHYDRATED FOOD PREPARATIONS	420	529	606	762	958	4.68	4.67
2035	PICKLES, SAUCES & SALAD DRESSINGS	818	920	987	1,110	1,248	2.37	2.38
2037	FROZEN FRUITS & VEGETABLES	1,012	1,481	1,862	2,726	3,991	7.92	7.93
2038	FROZEN SPECIALTIES	1,053	1,810	2,505	4,303	7,393	11.43	11.40

table 3-10

growth trend of product demand in customer industries
(sample printout: corrugated shipping containers—sic 2653)

CUSTOMER INDUSTRY		VALUE OF PURCHASES IN MILLIONS OF SQUARE FEET						
		ACTUAL			PROJECTED		ANNUAL GROWTH RATES	
SIC	DESCRIPTION	1967	1972	1975	1980	1985	67-72	72-75
2032	CANNED SPECIALTIES	1124.6	1600.8	1700.4	2011.7	2380.0	7.24	3.40
2033	CANNED FRUITS, VEGETABLES & JAMS	2563.3	3504.7	3722.7	4404.3	5210.7	6.42	3.43
2034	DEHYDRATED FOOD PREPARATIONS	349.7	499.7	530.2	627.3	742.2	7.43	3.42
2035	PICKLES, SAUCES & SALAD DRESSINGS	688.2	961.6	1021.4	1208.4	1429.6	6.96	3.44
2037	FROZEN FRUITS & VEGETABLES	875.0	1288.9	1369.1	1620.0	1916.6	8.12	3.41
2038	FROZEN SPECIALTIES	925.4	1407.5	1495.0	1768.7	2092.5	8.81	3.42

table 3-11

growth trends of product demand by state and county
(sample printout: corrugated shipping containers—sic 2653)

STATE COUNTY	NUMBER OF CUSTOMER PLANTS	VALUE OF PURCHASES IN MILLIONS OF SQUARE FEET				
		1967	1972	1975	1980	1985
ARKANSAS						
ARKANSAS	15	79,325	101,724	118,095	151,440	194,200
ASHLEY	14	42,176	52,058	59,066	72,905	89,987
BAXTER	5	5,322	6,506	7,340	8,973	10,970
BENTON	41	55,053	70,935	82,586	106,410	137,107
STATE TOTAL	792	1,877,086	1,978,850	2,083,524	2,187,700	2,296,350

46

Growth Trends of Product Demand by State and County (Table 3–11)

In this report the national totals shown in Table 3–9 are allocated to all states and counties on the basis of box demand in 1967, 1972, and 1975 as reflected in the EIS Databases of those years. For the projected years the allocation is based on the latest current EIS Database. This report will offer insights into regional growth patterns that add an important time dimension to the analysis of sales.

share of market for individual companies

A technical coefficient expressing the input requirement of any industry reflects the buy-sell transactions of all firms operating in that market. If plants in the glass container industry are buying corrugated boxes at the rate of $5,000 per employee, no producer of corrugated boxes could hope to sell boxes to any glass container plant at higher rates per employee. The actual percentage share of any given market enjoyed by a seller can vary between zero and 100 and can also differ widely from the producers' overall share of the national market, which can be easily calculated. A knowledge of the seller's share in any one market is of key importance in designing a sales strategy to increase "market penetration." One of the most effective uses of the EIS Database for any industrial seller is the calculation of his degree of market penetration, a procedure described by the next three tables.

These calculations depend on the so-called computer matching programs that compare a client's file of customers, and which can associate any given location in that file with the corresponding record in the EIS file. Matched client records are paired with the EIS counterpart record and are printed out in state-alpha-city sequence, while unmatched records are printed out in the same sequence on another file for clerical review. Table 3–12 illustrates a group of matched records. Client records that belong to multi-establishment companies will be successfully matched whether they appear under some variation or abbreviation of the parent name, or of a branch or subsidiary name (General Motors vs. Chevrolet, etc.). Table 3–13 summarizes the penetration ratios achieved by a client in all markets, and size groups, suitable for the analysis of untapped markets. Perhaps the most effective way to condense the information on market penetration would be in the form of a high-to-low listing of the largest potential customer *missing* from the client's customer list (Table 3–14), for here the first few pages can focus attention on the relatively few truly meaningful large potential accounts, particularly those that do not appear on customer invoices.

table 3–12
how customer records are matched to a database record

Acct. No.	Name of Customer	Address	City	State	ZIP	SIC	Total Employ-ment
15672	Grace, W.R. Chemed. Dv.	Central Express	Dallas	Tx.	75220		
23412	Du Bois Chemicals	South Central Expwy.	Dallas	Tx.	75222		
18911	W.R. Grace Division	8770 So. Central	Dallas	Tx.	75222		
36410	Du Bois Chem.	P.O. Box 22003	Dallas	Tx.	75222		
Database Record							
00045369	Du Bois Chem. Dv. W. R. Grace	8770 S. Central Expwy.	Dallas	42	75222	2841	75

Each of the first four records shown here are taken from a client's sales invoice file. Since each carries a different account number, it is evident that the sales clerk coding these invoices did not know that all referred to the same location. Despite the lack of discipline in spelling and nomenclature, these four records can be automatically matched to the bottom Database record, which carries the key information that Du Bois Chemicals belongs to W. R. Grace. The purpose of the match program is two-fold: to recognize duplicate invoice records, and to transfer Database information on industry and size to client sales invoice records in order to calculate market penetration.

corporate profitability and the managed penetration of industrial markets

The preceding tables have a bearing on how companies that sell to other companies can manage their investments in marketing. Modern corporate management is guided in its path to profits by a Return on Investment (ROI) concept, which states that investment requests should be approved if the projected returns meet predetermined criteria on quantity and quality of yield.

The concept has been applied successfully for many years in the manufacturing and technical spheres of companies where investments are typically made in tangible assets. For instance, a Vice-President of Engineering can request an investment to add a piece of machinery, and by using the manufacturer's specifications on the output of the machine (number of pieces the machine will produce per year) and the average price the new units will sell for, he can calculate the anticipated return on the investment in the new machine. By arraying all such requests for investment funds high-to-low in order of ROI, top management can readily select and approve those investments that will contribute most to profits.

Senior management, however, has generally not been able to apply this concept to industrial marketing even though there is general awareness that the yields on investments in industrial marketing have a far greater potential than comparable investments in manufacturing.

For instance, if a company has an industrial sales force of 100

table 3-13
market penetration analysis

Your Markets	Your Present Sales			The Full Market Potential		Your Present Market Share	
Defined by User Industries and Plant Size Class in Each Industry	You Now Sell to This Many Plants:	You Now Sell This Dollar Volume:	You Now Average This Dollar Volume Per Customer:	Number of Potential Customer Plants	Dollar Volume of Purchases by Those Plants	Buying Plants You Now Reach %	Dollar Volume You Now Achieve %
SIC 2812 Alkalies & Chlorine							
All Plants	14	90,400	6,457	40	513,200	35.0	21.5
Employs 20–49	4	15,600	3,900	5	24,500	80.0	63.7
50–99	3	20,400	6,800	5	26,000	60.0	78.4
100–249	2	10,000	5,000	13	110,400	15.4	9.1
250–499	2	10,000	5,000	7	112,200	28.5	8.9
500 +	3	34,400	11,466	10	240,000	30.0	14.3
SIC 3312 Steel Mills							
All Plants	13	74,806	12,843	255	4,257,200	5.1	1.8
Employs 20–49	5	3,750	750	28	28,000	17.9	13.3
50–99	4	4,460	1,115	18	25,200	22.2	17.7
100–249	1	9,876	9,876	38	380,000	2.6	2.6
250–499	1	11,200	11,200	41	574,000	2.4	2.0
500 +	2	44,800	22,400	130	3,250,000	1.5	1.4
Grand Total							
All Plants	1,618	9,351,480	5,779	12,136	90,881,800	13.3	10.3
Employs 20–49	480	1,506,200	3,138	3,782	3,650,400	12.6	41.3
50–99	324	2,116,400	6,487	2,654	6,710,600	12.2	31.5
100–249	256	1,249,280	4,880	2,015	18,420,100	12.7	6.8
250–499	216	1,017,200	4,709	1,933	24,600,500	11.1	4.1
500 +	342	3,462,400	10,124	1,752	37,500,200	19.5	9.2

table 3-14
high-low listing of corrugated box consumers (sic 2653) in louisiana

Rank-ing	SIC	Name	Address	City	State	ZIP	Phone Number	Total Employ-ment	Consump-tion, $	Cumu-lated %
1	3221	Owens Illinois	4300 Jourdan Rd./POB 26305	New Orleans	La.	70186	504-2412650	375	89,115	.04
2	3221	Underwood Glass Co. Inc.	P.O. Box 23188	New Orleans	La.	70123	504-7336755	250	59,410	.07
3	2822	Enjay Chemical Co.	P.O. Box 241	Baton Rouge	La.	70821	504-3597711	5000	56,750	.10
4	3221	Laurens Glass Company	P.O. Box 789	Simsboro	La.	71275	318-2556217	225	53,469	.13
5	2911	Humble Oil Refining Co.	P.O. Box 557	Baton Rouge	La.	70821	504-3597711	4000	44,040	.15
6	2087	Coca Cola Co.	123 Canal St.	New Orleans	La.	70130	504-8222400	300	43,569	.17
7	2641	Crown Zellerbach	Hwy. 61	St. Francisvil.	La.	70775	504-6353311	450	40,014*	.19
8	2062	Amstar Corp.	7417 North Peters	Arabi	La.	70032	504-5231071	875	39,978	.21
9	2062	Caire & Graungnard	P.O. Box 7	Edgard	La.	70049	504-4973351	800	36,552	.23
10	2082	Jackson Brewing Co. Inc.	620 Decatur	New Orleans	La.	70130	504-5237461	600	33,390	.25
11	2013	Joan of Arc Co.	Route 1 Box 164	Hessmer	La.	71341	318-5634586	400	33,336	.26
12	2621	Crown Zellerbach Corp.	Ave. S/P.O. Box 1060	Bogalusa	La.	70427	504-7322511	1500	30,225	.28
13	2079	Hunt Wesson Foods Inc.	Fourth St.	Gretna	La.	70053	504-3667261	180	30,135*	.30
14	2911	Cities Service Oil Co. Inc.	P.O. Box 1562	Lake Charles	La.	70601	318-4916011	2500	27,525	.31
15	2033	Princeville Canning Co.	Box 98A Rt. 1	Hessmer	La.	71341	318-5634587	700	24,521	.32
16	2621	International Paper Co.	705 Colliers La.	Bastrop	La.	71220	318-2811211	1200	24,180	.33
17	2062	Colonial Sugars Co. Inc.	129 S. 5th Ave.	Gramercy	La.	70052	504-8695521	500	22,845	.35
18	2062	Godchaux Henderson Sgr.	Jeff. Hwy.	Reserve	La.	70084	504-5361161	500	22,845	.36
19	2641	St. Francisville Paper Co.	Hwy. 61/P.O. Box 218	St. Francisvil.	La.	70775	504-6353311	250	22,230	.37
20	2821	Union Carbide Chem. Plastic	50 River Rd.	Taft	La.	70057	504-7836861	1000	21,040	.38
21	2033	B.F. Trappeys Sons Inc.	P.O. Box 2326	Lafayette	La.	70501	318-2320104	600	21,018	.39

In this listing, the two asterisks would indicate to a corrugated box manufacturer serving Louisiana that only two out of the top 21 are his customers, and that one of these, Crown Zellerbach, has another location, almost as important, which is not a customer.

**input/output databases
and technology**

men, each making 500 sales calls per year at an average price of $65 per call, the cost of maintaining this sales force will be $3.25 million per year (100 salesmen × 500 calls × $65). Assuming that 33% or $1.07 million of the sales calls are wasted, i.e., are made on prospects with absolutely no buying potential, and that the wasted sales calls can be reduced by 5 percentage points to 28%, the "savings" per year to the corporation would be 2,500 sales calls or $162,500 —not including the additional revenues the company would receive from the reallocation of the wasted 5% of sales calls to productive customers, which could provide an average value sale to each salesman.

Making the conservative assumption that the return on such an investment to upgrade sales call targets would be only $162,500, what size investment would be required to justify the return? In the manufacturing sphere, an investment for as much as $500,000 could probably be justified. In marketing, it would probably be possible to generate this return with an investment of no more than $70,000, through use of the computerized databases currently available.

Corporate management has generally been unable to exploit these investment opportunities because, until very recently, there has been no method of:

a. determining the number of sales calls that are being made on nonproductive prospects;
b. identifying the prospects that have sufficient buying potential to justify a sales call; and
c. measuring the success of the sales effort by measuring changes in market penetration.

The measure of change in market penetration is one of the key factors in determining if an investment in marketing is paying off. Until recently, market penetration measures for industrial companies were available only on a gross basis, i.e., the total output of the company versus the output of the industry to which the company belonged.*

It is now possible, with the aid of input/output analysis, to calculate and track a company's market penetration in every customer industry, every sales territory, and for every customer. It is also possible to determine if the prospects being called on have suffi-

---

*Measures of market penetration are widely used in consumer products marketing where hundreds of millions of dollars are typically spent each year to trace the changes in market standing of various products sold through retail channels, and to relate changes in market share in specific cities or for specific products to specific marketing projects such as television ads, newspaper ads, free samples coupons, and other "investments" in marketing.

cient buying potential to justify one sales call per week, per month, per quarter, or per year, or if the prospect should be contacted only by mail or phone. It is also possible to identify prospects who are *not* being called on, but who have sufficient buying power to justify systematic sales calls. And it is possible to identify prospects who can best be sold by distributors versus those who can best be sold direct.

For the first time, it is possible to answer such questions as the following:

—What return can I expect if I invest enough to increase the number of sales calls being made in a specific industry where I believe my market penetration can be increased from 10% to 15%—my average for all industries?

—What return can I expect if I invest enough to increase the number of sales calls in a territory where I believe my market penetration can be increased from 9% to 12%—a goal that appears to be reasonable in view of the buying potential of the territory?

—What return can I expect if I increase my marketing effort among the top "*Fortune* 500" companies so as to increase my market penetration among those buying units from 12% to 18%?

These questions could never be answered in the past because there was no reliable way of measuring existing market penetration for an industrial company and no way of measuring changes in market penetration on an ongoing basis. As we have seen, these problems have now been solved.

There is universal agreement that a company's market share is rarely held evenly in all markets and in all regions, so that the knowledge of how a company's market share varies from market to market and from region to region can lead to devising efficient marketing strategies for those markets requiring special efforts.

In order to determine industrial market penetration, a company must secure two pieces of information about each of its potential customers: how much, if any, of its product line was bought by that customer in a recent time period, and how much that customer bought from all sources. This is the familiar distinction between actual and potential sales, setting aside for the moment the key question of how to determine the potential.

The determination of actual sales (an element of the numerator in the market share ratio) generally presents no problem, as this information is available in the company's sales invoices, though

**input/output databases
and technology**

not without some data processing problems, as we shall see. But the truly new concept that is contributed by input/output economics is the concept of a "market potential" that exists for each firm if it could somehow "maximize" its sales to those prospects that would be most profitable to serve, either because they are volume buyers and the cost of sales to such accounts are low, or because they are in industries where their technical specifications permit production savings. It is this concept that will immediately spring to the mind of a sales manager who attempts to trace the flow of his product line to various markets as depicted in an input/output chart.

If the input/output chart were constructed at the desired level of detail, he would be able to tell how much of his product line flows to all major markets, arranged by industry and even by area. And if he were to reflect on the fact, let us say, that he knows that he accounts for only 10% of the total market, he is bound to wonder how his 10% market share would vary by market. He must speculate as to the relationship of his actual sales experience in each of his customer industries to all the numbers recorded on the input/output chart, which represent the total market size in each customer industry.

Many such questions came to mind when industrial sales managers and marketing executives eagerly studied the first input/output tables issued by the Department of Commerce in the 1950s and by the Department and *Scientific American* magazine in the '60s, but they could not be satisfactorily answered because data problems in those years required the use of broad market definitions that could rarely serve a specific market defined at least to the 4-digit level of the U.S. Standard Industrial Classification System (SIC).

Today, those data problems have essentially been solved. It is now possible to identify as many as 1,000 groupings of products and services that make up the vast bulk of the market for intermediate goods and services, bought by firms from other firms. The range of information on the estimated purchases of these firms, available for each of these separate entities, would have represented unrealizable hopes in the early days of input/output. Today the published input/output tables, although still useful for illustrative purposes and to indicate the logic of input/output, are, nevertheless, far more easy to manipulate in a computer rather than in published form.

The complexity of the data processing problem for measuring market penetration is highlighted by the fact that the system requires the generation of two establishment databases—one being a file of actual customer accounts based on sales invoices, and the other a file of all possible potential customer accounts taken from a public database.

We shall describe each file separately, in terms of its inner logic, and then consider the results of interfacing the two files. For purposes of exposition and illustration, we shall use the case of corrugated boxes, which represents a product line with one of the most diverse patterns of market demand, with more than 350 industries reporting some need for corrugated boxes as a packaging material.

Also, since most of the nation's top dozen producers of corrugated boxes have made use of one or more portions of the total system to be discussed below, such use of the system by this select group may offer some pragmatic validation of its usefulness.*

In an earlier section, "The Analysis of Current Industrial Demands," we found it useful to measure the technical coefficients as the dollars (or units) of input required per employee of the purchasing industry. Specifically, in 1975 some $4.4 billion of corrugated boxes were bought by 350 manufacturing industries employing some 15 million workers. Thus, on the average, each manufacturing employee required about $300 (equivalent to about 13,000 square feet) of corrugated boxes. But, of course, there is a great variation in the relative requirements of each 4-digit industry and the input/output coefficients enable us to calculate the approximate requirements of each. We have seen that after making our key assumption that within each 4-digit industry all plants share a common technology of production, then the computer can generate an estimate of the required input—in this case, corrugated boxes—for every potential customer. The information can then be arrayed and printed out in a wide variety of formats, in which special emphasis can be given in alternating combinations and permutations, to the industry of the plant, to its geographic location, or to its ultimate corporate owner.

In the next stage of analysis, it is necessary to compare or match the EIS Potential Database and a client's actual customer database in order to transfer to the latter the three key elements of EIS information—namely the SIC, the employment, and the potential sales volume for that location. This is done with the help of computer matching programs that "know" the ultimate corporate

---

*At this writing, for example, fourteen of the fifteen leading U.S. manufacturers of corrugated boxes have made use of some or all of these basic EIS reports in their analysis of sales.

parent of each location, and can seek the key letter sequences despite spelling variations (Table 3-12).*

After performing this function for several dozen clients, we have arrived at a remarkable evaluation. No client customer database is free of duplication unless it is small (under 1,000 accounts). The degree of duplication is of the order of 10% to 30% and increases with the number of accounts, probably reflecting the inability of clerks to cope with the permutations of nomenclature and spelling of business names and addresses in the business world. (It is estimated that there are over 30,000 permutations of the spelling of establishments belonging to the *"Fortune* 500" companies.) But the identification of duplication of sales accounts is merely one of many benefits for the sales manager who can now study the structure of his share of market in the most detailed manner possible.

Table 3-13, which summarizes a company's share of market in all regions, in all industries, and in all size groups, offers ample evidence of a wide range of variation from any single summary measure. In some regions a company may be able to trace a below-average performance to consistent biases in addressing plants with small potential or which are in the wrong industries—or to poor coverage of sales territory. Some sales regions hitherto thought to be well-performing, because in the past they have consistently reported greater than average sales gains (judged over time), may turn out to be operating below potential merely because an insufficient number of salesmen had been assigned to the region. Other sales regions thought to be performing poorly will prove to be providing a maximum attainable portion of the market potential in the region.

The reports that evaluate sales performance by comparing actual with potential sales can be generalized in a statistical sense (illustrated in Table 3-13) or they can be specific in terms of actual locations that should be called on (Table 3-14). They can be integrated into a series of periodic printouts designed to monitor and implement changes in sales tactics and strategy, and can be extended to include other measures of sales performance, such as number of calls and sales totaled so far this year, compared with last year. In other words, the sales potential data can now be integrated into a complete Management Information System, as promised in the early days of the computer age, but which is only now coming into being.

*The Cybernetics Division of Control Data Corporation offers realtime access to EIS matching programs in which the user retains control of his own sales data. This is an important consideration for companies that regard their sales data as far too sensitive to be sent outside their doors for processing.

A few observations may be offered on the way in which senior executives and sales managers have received the information about their market penetration from computerized databases and management information systems.

For the most part, the days are over, as compared to ten years ago, when line salesmen and sales managers challenged the market penetration and market potential results indicated by the computer. The ability of the computer to capture and organize hundreds of thousands of bits of data about the buying characteristics of customer industries, companies, and plants has virtually ended all subjective opposition to computerized reporting. The most rigid field tests and managerial scrutiny have proven that the quantity and quality of marketing data that can be captured by a computerized marketing system invariably exceeds the quantity and quality of data that can be dredged from the call reports, recollections, and interpretations of individual salesmen and sales managers, where varying degrees of sophistication, experience, and motivation provide built-in biases and inaccuracies.

The ability of a system to accept feedback from line salesmen upgrades the quality of marketing data and permits the database to be custom tailored to the needs of the users. Virtually every major company that addressed the problem of custom tailoring its database attempted to implement a well-structured information system that could accept new data and changes in data on an ongoing basis, and report the new data to the data bank users in a regular, systematic fashion. In this way, all changes in a company's market penetration could be tracked on a weekly or monthly basis, simultaneously with reporting of changes in company sales by region, product line, sales group, etc.

Senior management is becoming interested in ongoing reports of their market penetration by customer industry, sales territory, and national accounts prospects, so monitoring of marketing resources could be current with efforts in the field. In this way the benefits achieved from allocating marketing resources to specific projects could be measured continuously against the costs of resources utilized to achieve these goals.

In sum, for the handful of companies now using computerized databases and back-up information systems, the amounts of *usable* information made available about their market penetration and market potential have been substantial, and the returns on their investments have been quite high as compared to returns on investments of comparable size in tangible assets.

With this type of information at hand, the problems of determining where to "invest" in marketing becomes a top management problem that could be analyzed in terms of the cost/benefits that would result from every alternative course of action.

technology and competition

The reports described above, taken as a whole, can offer every manufacturer of a given product fairly complete information about his competitive position, and can even suggest the most efficient strategies for improving or extending his share of the market, in those markets where he feels he can make the most immediate gain. He may elect to do so by tapping what he believes is its growth potential over time, or its relatively unexploited current potential with respect to his particular type of product differentiation.

Theories of market competition generally assume that each buyer and seller has varying degrees of information based on the relative market power of all participants. Access to the EIS Database is thus seen to afford all producers a wide range of market information, regardless of the size of the company. There can be no question that the extended use of such databases can enhance competition.

In this context, it may be useful to review briefly the information chain on which the EIS Database capability rests, to emphasize that the huge information expansion triggered by the use of input/output technical coefficients obtained from Census tabulations does not violate the confidential character of data submitted by each company to the Census Bureau. The technical coefficients on which the EIS capability rests come from the Census reports on the purchases of buyers, but the purchases of individual establishments as reported to the Census Bureau are revealed only in aggregate form. These aggregates are then converted into estimates for each establishment. The information about each plant can then be portrayed in a multiplicity of formats with a resultant net information gain to all. In this process, no company gives up any proprietary information that can be used by competitors to its disadvantage.

The technical coefficients arrayed in an input/output table facilitate the analysis of the relationships between enterprises and industries, by focusing on the key factors that make for economic advance. Thus, one way in which a company can extend its share of any given market is to exploit any technical or marketing improvement or degree of product differentiation in a given market at the expense of its competitors. Innovations typically are not introduced across the board in all markets but are initially tested in those markets that appear most promising in the short run. Input/output statisticians thus acquire unique and powerful insights into the way in which technological innovations of all kinds begin and gradually pervade industrial processes.

These insights begin with an appreciation of the efficiency with which the Standard Industrial Classification System describes the multiplicity of technologies that make up a modern industrial economy, conveniently summarized at the 2-digit level into the twenty broad industrial groupings.

The various 4-digit industries can also be combined into broad groupings sharing similar basic technologies or processes. Since manufacturing can be defined as the mechanical or chemical transformation of organic or inorganic substances into new products, the following can be distinguished:

The Metal-Working Industries

There are over 200 metal-working industries to be found in the following 2-digit groups:

SIC	Name	Total Manufacturing Sales in 1972	
		$ Billion	%
25	Furniture products	11.3	1.5
33	Primary metals	58.4	7.7
34	Fabricated metal products	51.7	6.8
35	Nonelectrical machinery	65.8	8.7
36	Electrical machinery	53.4	7.1
37	Transportation equipment	94.7	12.5
38	Instruments and products	15.6	2.1
	Total	**350.9**	**46.4**
	Total Manufacturing—All SICs	**756.5**	**100.0**

All of these industries can require the following metal-working processes: foundry casting, forging, plating, galvanizing, heat treating, plate fabrication, stamping, blanking, metal forming, painting, lacquering, enameling, and plastics molding. They may, as a "make or buy" decision, operate screw machine departments, tool and die shops, or foundry pattern shops. In addition, they share common technological problems in the assembly and shipping of products.

The Chemical-Process Industries

There are about 200 other industries defined at the 4-digit level that are engaged in the chemical transformation of materials, falling into the following 2-digit groupings:

		Total Sales in 1972	
SIC	Name	$ Billion	%
20, 21	Food and tobacco	121.0	16.0
22	Textiles	28.1	3.7
26	Paper	28.3	3.7
28	Chemicals	57.3	7.6
29	Petroleum	28.7	3.8
30	Rubber and plastics	20.9	2.8
33	Primary metals	58.4	7.7
	Total	**342.7**	**45.3**
	Total Manufacturing—All SICs	**756.5**	**100.0**

Primary metals are included in the so-called CPI family because there is a heavy chemical-processing requirement in the manufacture of primary steel, aluminum, copper, zinc, and lead. Chemical-processing industries employ as basic technologies chemical synthesis and formulation, involving the mixing of chemicals by blending, emulsification, or solution. CPI technologies therefore tend to be highly automated, make heavy use of instrumentation in the measurement of the flow of liquids and gases, are heavy users of water, and are responsible for the bulk of environmental pollution problems.

Input-output statisticians can select many industrial products serving similar or related technological functions that can therefore be conveniently grouped together, even though they have different and unrelated SIC classifications and do not necessarily share a common technology of production.

The Packaging Industries

A good example is the family of about 40 packaging products, valued in the aggregate at about $25 billion in 1975. Table 3–15 lists these products on the vertical scale in the form of an abbreviated input-output table tracing the deliveries of these products to each manufacturing sector, defined (to save space) at the 2-digit SIC level. Even at this level of aggregation one can see how easily an input/output matrix can summarize, in less than $40 \times 20 = 800$ cells, all the markets in which packaging plays a role. The chief characteristics of packaging uses can be immediately discerned from the I/O table; Food, Chemicals and Drugs are evidently the major consumers because the relatively

table 3–15

structure of the u.s. packaging market ($ million)
(breakdown of consuming industries by sic no.)

Packaging products	SIC:	Ordnance 19	Food 20	Tobacco 21	Textiles 22	Apparel 23	Lumber and wood products 24	Furniture 25	Paper 26	Printing and publishing 27	Chemicals and drugs 28
Grocers' variety & misc. bags											
Specialty bags, paper & laminated			56.0	5.0							8.0
Glassine, waxed and parchment bags			25.6						3.8		1.6
Paper shipping sacks			103.7								111.2
Folding boxes		2.6	648.9	19.3	12.9	35.8			64.3	14.1	236.4
Rigid boxes			25.9		53.7	71.7			6.1	22.3	60.5
Molded pulp egg cartons											
Die-cut fillers for egg cases											
Sanitary food containers			765.0								
Fiber cans		6.0	72.3								18.3
Fiber drums			16.0						.3		79.2
Corrugated shipping containers		21.0	855.7	20.9	79.1	38.4	12.9	110.1	390.2	48.3	217.4
Flexible paper & paper combination			225.0	2.0	10.0	4.0		3.0	21.0	5.0	15.0
Cigarette & gum wraps			12.0	100.0							
Cellophane			170.0	42.5					5.5		7.0
Polyethylene			391.9		18.0	45.1			129.4	4.6	7.7
Metal foil, flexible			55.0	13.4							6.7
Metal cans, except aerosol			3572.8	20.3							162.4
Aerosols			26.8								434.2
Collapsible metal tubes		.1	58.7								
Foil containers, rigid & semi-rigid			55.5								
Steel shipping barrels, drums, pails			23.4								368.8
Steel strapping		3.6			4.3	2.1	2.7	6.9	5.3		
Gas cylinders		.2									56.4
Glass containers			1468.4								316.3
Closures			381.3	.1							120.6
Plastic bottles			70.7								353.8
Plastic boxes & baskets			7.1								34.3
Plastic tubes											39.4
Plastic jars & tubs			34.0								34.0
Plastic sheet, rigid & semi-rigid			10.0								30.0
Foamed plastics		2.0						5.0			5.0
Wooden containers		8.2	134.9	7.7	.2		22.0	1.7	.8	.1	13.4
Textile bags			88.2								13.9
Cushioning materials		2.0						4.0			
Adhesives			7.0						100.0		
Labels & tags		1.2	300.4	3.9	9.0	45.0	.6	5.2	10.0	4.1	67.3
Pressure sensitive & gummed tape		1.2	52.4	1.2	4.8	2.4	.8	6.8	23.8	3.0	13.2
Twine					3.0	3.0		2.0		2.0	
Cargo or bulk containers		1.0	.6	.1	.4		.2	.2	.2		6.1
Total		**49.1**	**9715.2**	**236.4**	**195.4**	**247.6**	**39.2**	**144.9**	**760.7**	**103.5**	**2838.1**

Petroleum 29	Rubber and plastics 30	Leather 31	Stone, clay glass 32	Primary metals 33	Metal products 34	Machinery 35	Electrical equipment 36	Transportation 37	Instruments 38	Miscellaneous mfg. 39	Total mfg.	Service sectors	Grand total
												390.0	390.0
					1.0				2.0	3.0	75.0	15.0	90.0
					.3		.3				31.6	.4	32.0
1.6			67.9							2.8	287.2	72.8	360.0
	12.9	11.6	23.1	12.9	45.0		16.7	12.9	6.4	45.0	1220.8	79.2	1300.0
	4.3	17.3	6.1		6.1				30.4	60.6	365.0	67.0	432.0
												109.0	109.0
												22.0	22.0
											765.0	510.0	1275.0
68.4	.9									5.1	171.0	10.0	181.0
2.0			3.4	3.2	1.2						105.3	6.7	112.0
31.3	128.7	18.0	352.9	41.6	163.1	81.8	227.5	117.8	33.3	280.8	3270.8	404.2	3675.0
	2.0				2.0	2.0	2.0		2.0	5.0	300.0	80.0	380.0
											112.0		112.0
											225.0	25.0	250.0
	5.4	3.9			18.5		2.3			10.0	636.8	133.2	770.0
									6.0	.4	81.5	.5	82.0
81.2									20.3		3857.0	203.0	4060.0
											461.0		461.0
	.7				.1					.4	60.0		60.0
											55.5	22.5	78.0
47.0	4.0		2.8		37.5	.4		.1			584.0	24.0	608.0
	2.7	3.4	30.3	6.4	28.5	32.0	29.5		3.7		161.4	12.6	174.0
1.0				.2	.5	3.9	3.0	.5	.3	.8	66.8	17.2	84.0
2.7					1.6				9.7	23.3	1822.0	278.0	2100.0
.8	1.5				.4				1.4	3.7	509.8	16.2	526.0
2.6									.4		427.5	.5	428.0
					13.8	4.9	18.0		15.0	20.7	113.8	10.2	124.0
	.3									.2	39.9		40.0
											68.0		68.0
	5.0				10.0				5.0	30.0	90.0	11.0	101.0
			5.0			4.0	15.0		4.0		40.0	9.0	49.0
.3	5.0	4.5	20.6	7.7	25.7	30.7	31.3	17.2	3.5	4.6	340.1	231.9	572.0
			18.4	2.1	11.1						133.7	57.3	191.0
			9.0		2.0	3.0	5.0		5.0	1.0	31.0	2.0	33.0
	1.5										108.5	1.5	110.0
5.2	7.0	3.3	5.0	2.3	10.4	4.0	11.6	1.5	4.6	22.0	523.6	56.4	580.0
2.0	7.8	1.2	21.6	2.6	10.0	5.0	14.0	7.2	2.0	17.0	200.0	170.0	370.0
											10.0	54.0	64.0
1.1	.4		.4	2.1	.5	.1	.2				13.6	276.4	290.0
347.2	190.1	63.2	566.5	81.1	389.3	171.8	376.4	157.2	155.0	536.4	17364.3	3378.7	20743.0

high unit value of these products warrants the use of large quantities and varieties of packaging materials. Again, technological factors clearly explain, for example, why steel shipping barrels, drums, and pails flow so heavily to the Chemicals and Petroleum industries or why wood containers are heavily bought by Tobacco manufacturers.

Another important industrial family is represented by the makers of equipment designed to handle materials: industrial tractors, forklift trucks, conveyor belts, overhead hoists and cranes, etc. A close technological connection can be discerned between packaging products and materials handling, helpful to the input/output statistician in projecting end-use consumption patterns of products and services based on their industrial function. For example, makers of conveyor belts and of multiwall shipping sacks serve some of the same markets: processors of dry porous bulk materials like flour, sugar, salt, cement, etc.

To take full advantage of such technological correlations, an input/output statistician should have an engineering background and an understanding of industrial technology. Then, for any new product or service with a well-defined industrial function, the statistician can select all potential consuming industries. Relative weights can then be assigned to each industry, often on the basis of the known consumption pattern of other products serving similar functions.

Tables 3–16 and 3–17 offer additional summaries of end-use consumption patterns for industrial fasteners and power transmission equipment. Industrial fasteners include various kinds of threaded and unthreaded screws, bolts, nuts, rivets, washers, etc., almost all flowing to the metal-working industries.

Power transmission equipment refers to the full range of components, assemblies, and accessory devices affecting the linkage and control of power between the prime mover and driven machine. Thus the term covers such mechanical components as gears, couplings, drive chains, belts, pulleys; fluid power components (pneumatic and hydraulic valves, cylinders, motors, line accessories); and mechanical and fluid power drive assemblies (speed changers, clutches, brakes, transmissions).

These are only a few of several product groupings of highly specialized products of interest particularly to industrial wholesalers. Industrial distributors offer an important service to both small and large manufacturers, in minimizing the inherently high cost of marketing specialized technical products to sophisticated buyers. The industrial distributor, serving a limited geographic area, can thus be seen to play a key role in the transmission and dissemina-

table 3–16
purchases of fastener products, 1974
($ million)

SIC		Heavy Threaded	Light Threaded	Wood & Sheet Metal Screw	Non-Threaded	Total	% Use by industry
19	Ordnance	19.9	3.9	.3	8.1	32.2	2.1
20	Food	.5				.5	
21	Tobacco						
22	Textiles	.2				.2	
23	Apparel, Furnishings						
24	Wood Products	3.0	1.4	5.0	1.2	10.6	.7
25	Furniture, Fixtures	16.8	4.8	21.8	5.7	49.1	3.1
26	Paper Products	1.5			.2	1.7	.1
27	Printing				.6	.6	
28	Chemicals, Resins	2.8	.3		.4	3.5	.3
29	Oil Products	2.2	.2		.3	2.7	.2
30	Plastics, Rubber	1.4	2.9	5.8	1.8	11.9	.8
31	Leather Products				8.8	8.8	.6
32	Mineral Products	.3				.3	
33	Primary Metals	31.9	3.4	4.9	29.6	69.8	4.4
34	Fabricated Metals	128.6	25.7	36.6	59.4	250.3	15.9
35	Machinery	174.0	21.6	27.5	78.2	301.3	19.2
36	Electrical, Appliances	113.2	40.2	62.8	99.3	315.5	20.1
37	Transportation Equip.	278.3	34.4	45.9	75.5	434.1	27.6
38	Instruments	9.1	19.5	18.2	.8	54.9	3.5
39	Misc. Mfg.	6.2	5.0	6.6	4.2	22.0	1.4
	Total MFG Consumption	789.9	163.3	235.4	381.4	1570.0	100.0
	Non-Mfg. Use Including Construction	358.8	33.5	48.2	159.5	600.0	
	Total U.S. Consumption	1140.7	196.8	283.6	540.9	2170.0	

tion of technological innovations, which usually center on products of great technical specificity, of concern to small numbers of key buyers. In the performance of his function, the industrial distributor divides his customers into the original equipment manufacturers who are buying components, and those who buy industrial equipment and supplies (in far smaller quantities) for maintenance and replacement.

63

table 3-17.

industry's purchases of power transmission equipment ($ million), 1976

SIC		Components Mechanical & Electrical	Fluid Power	Assemblies Mechanical & Electrical	Fluid Power	Totals
20	Food	17.2	3.7	23.4	8.0	52.3
21	Tobacco	0.9	0.2	0.7	2.3	4.1
22	Textiles	11.8	2.9	11.7	5.2	31.6
23	Apparel, Furnishings	0.5	0.1	0.3	0.1	1.0
24	Wood Products	8.8	2.0	6.4	1.8	19.0
25	Furniture, Fixtures	4.3	0.8	2.9	0.6	8.6
26	Paper Products	28.0	17.1	47.8	25.0	117.9
27	Printing	7.5	1.7	10.9	2.1	22.2
28	Chemicals, Resins	23.2	28.4	90.9	25.0	167.5
29	Oil Products	12.9	6.8	15.3	4.5	39.5
30	Plastics & Rubber	5.2	14.3	15.8	4.4	39.7
31	Leather Products	0.9	0.2	1.2	0.3	2.6
32	Mineral Products	16.3	6.1	23.1	13.9	59.4
33	Primary Metals	44.5	50.6	92.0	26.8	213.9
34	Fabricated Metals	42.0	44.1	32.4	7.6	126.1
35	Machinery	1,661.0	874.0	266.0	68.9	2,869.9
36	Electricals, Appliances	251.0	78.8	31.2	11.0	372.0
37	Transportation Equipment	329.0	246.0	96.1	20.5	691.6
38	Instruments, Controls	30.2	25.5	8.5	1.6	65.8
39	Misc. Manufacturing	4.8	0.9	3.4	0.4	9.5
Total Manufacturing Use		**2,500.0**	**1,404.2**	**780.0**	**230.0**	**4,914.2**
Net Export and Nonmanufacturing Use*		**531.0**	**373.0**	**222.0**	**76.0**	**1,202.0**
Total U.S. Production		**3,031.0**	**1,777.2**	**1,002.0**	**306.0**	**6,116.2**

*Nonmanufacturing markets include mining, construction, power utilities, and servicing aftermarkets

the nature of technological advance

The specialized nature of industrial demand makes it difficult for any radically new innovation to achieve immediate dominance in all markets. A long period of testing, market by market, is necessary to adapt the innovation to the specific requirements of each market.

The postwar emergence of plastics as a basic industrial material, for example, took three decades to reach peak levels: the production in 1976 of 22 billion pounds valued at $15 billion. And as proof of the necessity for specialized market adaptation, two-thirds of all plastic resins today are bought by manufacturers for "captive" processing. Thus, most heavy users of plastics prefer, as a "make or buy" decision, to purchase plastics processing

input/output databases and technology

equipment to permit them to engage in secondary plastics processing activity that is tied to the special requirements of the primary operations of a given plant. This is in direct contrast to the industrial use of rubber, where we find comparatively little captive rubber processing.

An even more far-reaching change in industrial technology is now underway, involving the application of recent advances in solid state electronics to both the automation of production and the purchase of microprocessors and minicomputers by original equipment manufacturers, which can greatly extend the capacity and flexibility of industrial equipment of all kinds.

While it is difficult to measure technical advance in the short run,

table 3–18
employment of scientists, engineers, and technicians in manufacturing, 1970

SIC	Industry	1970 Total Employ- ment	Technical Labor Force (000)						Tech- nical Index
			% of Total	Total	Engin- eers	Scient- ists	Techni- cians	% of Total	
19	Ordnance	323	1.8	68.7	45.4	7.1	16.2	5.9	328
20, 21	Food & Tobacco	1,710	9.3	21.3	7.7	7.5	6.1	1.8	19
22	Textile Products	922	5.0	8.9	3.9	2.0	3.0	0.8	16
23	Apparel	1,330	7.3	2.3	—	—	—	0.2	3
24	Lumber & Wood	545	3.0	3.5	—	—	—	0.3	10
25	Furniture	434	2.4	3.5	—	—	—	0.3	13
26	Paper	657	3.6	22.0	—	—	—	1.9	53
27	Printing & Publishing	1,081	5.9	5.8	—	—	—	0.5	9
28	Chemicals	878	4.8	154.1	46.4	60.9	46.8	13.3	277
29	Petroleum	146	0.8	19.7	9.2	4.0	6.5	1.7	213
30	Rubber & Plastics	548	3.0	20.9	11.0	4.1	5.8	1.8	60
31	Leather Products	296	1.6	1.1	—	—	—	0.1	6
32	Stone, Glass, Clay	595	3.2	19.5	9.8	2.5	7.2	1.7	53
33	Primary Metals	1,260	6.9	50.4	19.6	10.2	20.6	4.4	63
34	Fabricated Metals	1,337	7.3	56.0	27.6	2.6	25.8	4.8	66
35	Machinery, Nonelectric	1,890	10.3	172.3	85.1	9.0	78.2	14.9	145
36	Electrical Machinery	1,840	10.0	273.6	149.0	14.4	110.2	23.7	237
37	Transportation Equipment	1,686	9.2	189.3	120.2	11.5	57.6	16.4	178
38	Instruments	404	2.2	60.9	31.5	6.0	23.4	5.3	240
39	Miscellaneous	430	2.3	2.3	—	—	—	0.2	9
	Total	**18,312**	**100.0**	**1,155.7**	**583.1**	**149.8**	**422.8**	**100.0**	**100**

Source: National Science Foundation and 1970 Survey of Manufactures

table 3–19
productivity changes in manufacturing, 1947–1970

SIC	Industry	1970 Value added ($ billion)	1970 Value added per employee ($ thousand)	1947 Value added per employee ($ thousand)	Ratio of Change	Index of Productivity Change
19	Ordnance	5.1	15.8	4.6	3.40	109
20, 21	Food & Tobacco	34.3	20.0	6.3	3.15	101
22	Textile Products	9.3	10.1	4.3	2.32	74
23	Apparel	11.6	8.7	4.1	2.17	69
24	Lumber & Wood	5.9	10.8	3.9	2.75	88
25	Furniture	4.8	11.1	4.3	2.58	82
26	Paper	11.5	17.5	6.4	2.73	87
27	Printing & Publishing	17.3	16.0	5.9	2.71	87
28	Chemicals	27.9	31.8	8.5	3.74	119
29	Petroleum	5.4	37.0	9.6	3.87	124
30	Rubber & Plastics	8.5	15.5	5.0	3.07	98
31	Leather Products	2.8	9.5	4.0	2.37	76
32	Stone, Glass, Clay	9.9	16.6	5.0	3.32	106
33	Primary Metals	21.4	17.0	5.0	3.40	109
34	Fabricated Metals	20.7	15.5	5.1	3.07	98
35	Machinery, Non-electric	31.8	16.8	5.0	3.33	106
36	Electrical Machinery	27.8	15.1	4.8	3.14	101
37	Transportation Equipment	28.9	17.1	5.0	3.43	110
38	Instruments	7.9	19.6	4.7	4.20	134
39	Miscellaneous	5.5	12.8	4.5	2.87	92
	Total	**298.3**	**16.3**	**5.2**	**3.13**	**100**

Source: Census of Manufactures, 1970, 1947

over the long term productivity gains remain the best single indicator of the advance of technology. Since the turn of the century output per man in manufacturing has increased at the fairly uniform rate of 2.5% per year. The number of manufacturing workers has remained, however, at the level of about 20 million throughout the postwar years. Consequently a radical occupational shift has occurred in the manufacturing work force, with the gradual replacement of unskilled production workers by salaried technicians.

In 1970, the employment of scientists, engineers, and technicians in manufacturing numbered 1,156,000 in a national technical work force of 1.6 million, according to data collected by the

table 3–20
high-salaried employees in manufacturing, 1970
breakdown by industry

SIC	Industry	$15,000 per year (000)	%	Earning Over $20,000 per year (000)	%	$25,000 per year (000)	%
19	Ordnance	39.1	3.2	20.8	2.6	10.5	2.1
20, 21	Food & Tobacco	58.9	4.8	41.6	5.2	29.5	5.9
22	Textile Products	24.5	2.0	16.8	2.1	10.5	2.1
23	Apparel	35.3	2.8	20.0	2.5	8.4	1.7
24	Lumber & Wood	20.8	1.7	12.8	1.6	7.4	1.5
25	Furniture	16.9	1.4	11.2	1.4	6.8	1.4
26	Paper	33.3	2.7	21.6	2.7	14.2	2.8
27	Printing & Publishing	87.7	7.1	48.0	6.0	26.3	5.3
28	Chemicals	98.1	7.9	75.0	9.4	48.7	9.7
29	Petroleum	24.4	1.9	19.4	2.4	12.5	2.5
30	Rubber & Plastics	24.4	1.9	16.8	2.1	11.9	2.3
31	Leather Products	4.4	0.4	4.0	0.5	3.3	0.5
32	Stone, Glass, Clay	28.7	2.3	18.4	2.3	11.6	2.3
33	Primary Metals	58.2	4.7	38.4	4.8	25.0	5.0
34	Fabricated Metals	71.9	5.8	48.8	6.1	31.6	6.3
35	Machinery, Non-electric	160.6	13.0	109.6	13.7	69.5	13.9
36	Electrical Machinery	146.3	11.8	100.3	12.6	63.2	12.6
37	Transportation Equipment	187.4	15.1	120.0	15.1	73.8	14.8
38	Instruments	34.7	2.8	28.0	3.5	19.5	3.9
39	Miscellaneous	83.5	6.8	28.1	3.6	15.8	3.4
	Total	**1,239.0**	**100.0**	**800.6**	**100.0**	**500.0**	**100.0**

Source: Census of 1970

National Science Foundation.* The distribution of this technical work force into 2-digit SIC manufacturing sectors is indicated in Table 3–18, and is expressed as a relative called an Index of

*An interesting story lies behind these figures. In a previous study of the impact of science on industry, entitled *The Technical Elite,* published by A. M. Kelley in New York in 1966, I was able to measure the steady exponential growth of the technical work force for the period 1900–1960 with decennial Census data on occupations. With a bit of historical research I found that it was possible to extrapolate this series back to its literal point of origin, when Ben Franklin could be said to be the first American to be fully engaged in scientific and technical work. I found that both the historical estimates and the Census data fell precisely on a logarithmic parabola that reached a total of 3.5 million in the year 2000. I have reproduced this chart exactly as it was printed in 1966 with the observation that the curve "predicted" a technical work force of 1.7 million for 1970, slightly above the NSF figure. The predicted value for 1980 is 2.1 million (Table 3–22).

table 3–21
relation of technical employment to productivity and high income

SIC	Industry	Index of Technical Employment 1970	Index of High Income 1970	Index of Productivity 1970
19	Ordnance	328	144	109
28	Chemicals	277	196	119
38	Instruments	240	159	134
36	Electrical Machinery	237	126	100
29	Petroleum Products	213	300	124
37	Transportation Equipment	178	164	110
35	Machinery	145	133	106
34	Fabricated Metals	66	78	98
33	Primary Metals	63	70	109
30	Rubber	60	70	98
26	Paper	53	75	87
32	Stone, Clay, Glass	53	71	106
20, 21	Food & Tobacco	19	56	101
22	Textiles	16	42	74
25	Furniture	13	53	82
24	Lumber & Wood	10	53	88
31	Leather	6	31	76
23	Apparel	3	34	69
	Total	**100**	**100**	**100**

Technical Employment. Note that the highest indexes characterize, in order, Ordnance (merged into other sectors after 1972), Chemicals, Instruments, Electrical Machinery, and Petroleum.

In Tables 3–19, 3–20, and 3–21 there is assembled the evidence necessary to show a high correlation of the Index of Technical Employment to growth in value-added per worker over the 1947–1970 period, and to the incidence of salaried employees earning over $20,000 in 1970. With respect to all these indicators, the industrial sectors with above-average scores are Ordnance, Chemicals, Instruments, Electrical Machinery, Petroleum Products, Transportation Equipment, and Machinery, Nonelectric. At the 4-digit level of SIC detail, the correlation would be even more pronounced. Industries such as SIC 2869 (Organic Chemicals), SIC 2911 (Petroleum Refining), and SIC 3573 (Computers and Related Equipment) have technical employment percentages greater than 25% and correspondingly lead in growth of income and productivity.

With the further extension of the computer to industrial automa-

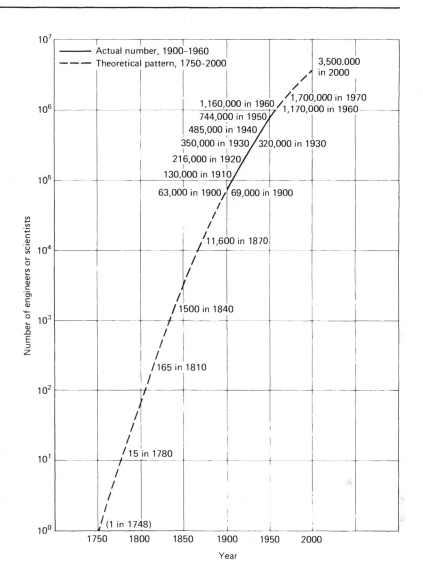

tion, we can in the future expect great productivity gains in such hitherto labor intensive industries as typesetting, printing, food processing, and apparel manufacturing.

For the input/output statistician, these and other slow and steady changes of technology should be studied at the most detailed level possible: in the various markets ruled by their technical coefficients.

chapter 4

a database analysis of concentration in u.s. business

In Chapter 2 we used as a measure of aggregate concentration of U.S. enterprise the fact that the leading 2,500 companies accounted for 64% of total corporate sales. The subject of concentration lies at the heart of weighty economic questions concerning the growth, efficiency, profitability, and pricing policies of American business. The Database studies of concentration discussed below have been prepared for both business and government use, and can often be used by both sides in public and private antitrust litigation.

In this context, a definitive analysis of concentration can be found in John M. Blair's *Economic Concentration: Structure, Behavior and Public Policy*.* We have adopted much of Dr. Blair's analytical framework here, but will not attempt to repeat or summarize his insights or findings beyond concurring in the emphasis he gives to the problem. We shall instead try to sketch areas in which use of the EIS Database can extend the study of concentration and help resolve questions that have hitherto gone unanswered.

*Dr. Blair, as chief economist for the Senate Anti-Trust Committee over a period of three decades, extending back to the pre-war TNEC hearings on the Concentration of Economic Power, was a lifelong student of concentration and monopoly and was a leading force in the elaboration of the statistical procedures required of the Census Bureau to analyze concentration, such as the publication of the share of sales of the top four, eight, and twenty companies in each 4-digit manufacturing industry.

market concentration

How widespread is concentration in American business? In Table 4–1 a breakdown is given of the sales of the top 2,500 companies accounting for 64% of total corporate sales by 2-digit sectors. If we regard as "concentrated" those sectors in which these companies account for half or more of total sales, all the mining sectors and all the manufacturing sectors with the exception of Apparel, Lumber, Furniture, Printing and Publishing, Leather, Fabricated Metals, and Miscellaneous Manufacturing must be included in this category. (Concentration appears to be correlated with high technical employment and productivity gains.) As would be expected in the nonmanufacturing sectors, concentration characterizes the regulated transportation, power and communication utilities, and insurance and food and drug retailing. In general, however, the trades and service sectors are *not* concentrated in this sense.

Market concentration can be best measured when a market is as narrowly defined as possible—i.e. at the 4-digit SIC level—and is dominated by a small number of producers. With respect to the concentration ratios published by the Census Bureau, a 4-digit industry can be said to be concentrated when the top four companies account for 50% or more of total output. Such ratios can be periodically checked against corresponding estimates from the EIS file except that company identities can now be revealed.

table 4–1
breakdown of sales of top 2,500 companies by 2-digit sic sectors, 1976 (billion $)

SIC	Industry	Total Sector Sales ($ Billion)	Sales, Top 2,500	% of Total
01	Crop Production	4,358	1,966	45
02	Livestock Production	2,876	754	26
07	Agricultural Services	1,301	304	23
08	Forestry	91	31	34
10	Metal Mining	4,798	3,835	79
11	Anthracite Mining	248	0	0
12	Bituminous Coal & Lignite Mining	8,677	6,258	72
13	Oil & Gas Extraction	46,298	34,771	75
14	Nonmetallic Minerals, exc. Fuels	4,608	2,362	51
15	General Building Contractors	37,620	10,403	27
16	Heavy Construction Contractors	23,084	9,034	39
17	Special Trade Contractors	17,077	1,534	8
20	Food & Kindred Products	196,445	116,313	59
21	Tobacco Manufacturers	10,977	9,844	89
22	Textile Mill Products	41,239	19,623	47
23	Apparel & Other Textile Products	39,256	9,990	25

Continued

SIC	Industry	Total Sector Sales ($ Billion)	Sales, Top 2,500	% of Total
24	Lumber & Wood Products	29,986	10,626	35
25	Furniture & Fixtures	16,316	4,526	27
26	Paper & Allied Products	46,426	34,632	74
27	Printing & Publishing	44,438	17,476	39
28	Chemicals & Allied Products	117,108	94,579	80
29	Petroleum & Coal Products	61,167	55,764	91
30	Rubber & Miscellaneous Plastics Products	30,606	14,271	46
31	Leather & Leather Products	8,898	2,939	33
32	Stone, Clay & Glass Products	31,702	16,724	52
33	Primary Metal Industries	76,967	58,877	76
34	Fabricated Metal Products	81,016	36,375	44
35	Machinery, Non-electrical	108,940	65,784	60
36	Electric & Electronic Equipment	72,987	50,966	69
37	Transportation Equipment	100,459	86,922	86
38	Instruments & Related Products	26,054	16,424	63
39	Miscellaneous Manufacturing	18,450	6,217	33
40	Railroad Transportation	15,404	14,596	94
41	Local & Interurban Passenger Transit	2,467	1,404	56
42	Trucking & Warehousing	25,535	11,588	45
43	U.S. Postal Service	1,086	1,086	100
44	Water Transportation	6,662	5,313	79
45	Transportation by Air	16,879	15,838	93
46	Pipe Lines, exc. Natural Gas	6,634	6,255	94
47	Transportation Services	5,427	3,197	58
48	Communication	28,287	25,176	89
49	Electric, Gas & Sanitary Services	81,473	69,912	85
50	Wholesale Trade—Durable Goods	160,063	53,092	33
51	Wholesale Trade—Nondurable Goods	270,144	125,936	46
52	Building Materials & Garden Supplies	18,664	2,650	14
53	General Merchandise Stores	82,205	69,754	84
54	Food Stores	78,322	64,105	81
55	Automotive Dealers & Service Stations	57,561	11,104	19
56	Apparel & Accessory Stores	16,508	5,538	33
59	Miscellaneous Retail	37,674	20,252	53
60, 61	Banking, Credit Agencies	46,535	41,857	90
62	Security, Commodity Brokers & Services	8,845	4,942	55
63, 64	Insurance	101,662	81,299	80
65, 66	Real Estate	13,906	4,477	32
67	Holding Companies	95,068	75,908	79
70	Hotels & Other Lodging Places	6,693	2,692	40
72	Personal Services	3,279	608	18
73	Business Services	33,410	19,370	57

Continued

SIC	Industry	Total Sector Sales ($ Billion)	Sales, Top 2,500	% of Total
75	Auto Repair, Services & Garages	5,328	2,384	44
76	Miscellaneous Repair Services	1,307	560	42
78	Motion Pictures	3,446	2,484	72
79	Amusement & Recreation Services	2,340	1,096	46
80	Health Services	1,668	555	33
81	Legal Services	113	109	96
82	Educational Services	213	43	20
83	Social Services	22	0	0
84	Museums, Botanical, Zoological Gardens	9	0	0
86	Membership Organizations	158	0	0
89	Miscellaneous Services	29,398	10,582	35
	Totals	**2,601,291**	**1,564,770**	**60**

For every 4-digit industry an EIS Share-of-Market Report can be prepared as in Table 4–2 in which each company in a given industry is listed in the order of total sales generated in that industry by all plants owned by the company and classified in that industry. Sales percentages are cumulated so that one can note the share accounted for any number of leading companies. In the case of Table 4–2, SIC 3743 (Railroad Equipment), for example, the latest (1972) Census of Manufactures data assigns a concentration ratio of 56% to the top four companies in this industry, and 70% to the top eight. In the corresponding EIS Share-of-Market Report the top four companies are seen to account for 55.4% and the top eight for 74.6%. Although the correspondence is only approximate, it seems clear that both sets of figures reflect the same underlying reality.

It is instructive to note that the accuracy of the EIS estimates rests heavily on a small number of very large plants, whose precise size is withheld in published Census tables. But the employment of the General Electric locomotive plant in Erie, Pennsylvania, is cited as 7,400 in a recent Pennsylvania directory, and the employment of the General Motors locomotive plant in McCook, Illinois, is given as 8,000 in a recent Illinois directory. These two plants alone account for 32% of total industry employment and thus must command the attention of any serious student of the industry.

table 4-2
share of market report for sic 3743 railroad equipment

Rank	Parent Company Branch Plants	Address	City	State	ZIP	Telephone Number	Estimated 1976 Sales ($ Million)	Share of Market (% U.S.)	Cumulated Share of Market
1	General Motors Corp.	767 Fifth Avenue	New York	N.Y.	10022	212-4865000	648.4	17.19	17.19
	Electro Motive Div. GM	3545 New Kings Rd.	Jacksonville	Fl.	32203	904-7651611	6.2	.17	
	Electro Motive Div. GM	900 E. 103rd St.	Chicago	Il.	60628	312-WA81200	78.5	2.08	
	Electro Motive Div. GM	9301 55th St.	Mc Cook	Il.	60529	312-4857000	557.2	14.76	
	Electro Motive Div. GM	4701 Washington	Halethorpe	Md.	21227	301-2424450	6.5	.18	
2	General Electric Co.	3135 Easton Tpke.	Fairfield	Ct.	06430	203-3732211	640.0	16.95	34.14
	General Electric Co.	2901 East Lake Rd.	Erie	Pa.	16501	814-4555466	640.0	16.95	
3	Pullman Incorporated	200 S. Michigan Ave.	Chicago	Il.	60604	312-9394262	530.5	14.05	48.19
	Pullman-Standard Inc.	5th Ave. & 24th St./Box 428	Bessemer	Al.	35020	205-4253231	109.7	2.90	
	Pullman-Standard	1745 165th St.	Hammond	In.	46320	219-9323280	74.9	1.99	
	Pullman Inc.	Hansen Ave.	Butler	Pa.	16001	215-2875765	345.9	9.16	
4	ACF Industries Inc.	750 3rd Ave.	New York	N.Y.	10017	212-9868600	271.8	7.20	55.39
	ACF Indus-Amcar Div.	2800 Dekalb St.	St. Louis	Mo.	63118	314-7738870	164.8	4.37	
	ACF Indus-Amcar Div.	2nd & Arch Sts.	Milton	Pa.	17847	717-7427601	45.7	1.21	
	ACF Industries-Amcar Div.	2300 Third Ave./Box 547	Huntington	Wv.	25710	304-5293211	61.3	1.62	

regional
concentration

In some markets for nondurable goods, the national ratios understate the true extent of concentration. A good example is SIC 2051 (Bread and Related Products). Here the 1972 Census 4-company ratio is 29%. A recent EIS Share-of-Market Report for this industry carries a 4-company ratio of only 26%, in part because of the difficulty of achieving complete coverage of all relatively small regional bakeries. (ITT-Continental Bakers, the industry leader, has over 70 such plants.)

Regional variation in concentration can be studied in the EIS Shipments Reports prepared for each industry (see Table 4–3), in which the plant and establishment data are arranged alphabetically in state and county sequence.* Here, for example, are how the 4-company ratios would look for leading metropolitan areas:

New York Metropolitan Counties	21.46%
Chicago Metropolitan Counties	15.84
Los Angeles Metropolitan Counties	32.30
Cincinnati Metropolitan Counties	67.06
Kansas City, Missouri, Metropolitan Counties	86.76
San Francisco Metropolitan Counties	47.72

Source: EIS Shipments Reports, SIC 2051, Bread, Cake, and Related Products

concentration and
profitability

That there is a high correlation between concentration and profitability has been repeatedly established by many investigators in recent years. The only problem, as Blair has observed, is that as the statistical techniques for such demonstrations get increasingly more sophisticated, the available financial data from which the profit rates are drawn have become progressively less usable. Continuing waves of mergers and acquisitions alter the structure of large corporations making it more difficult to assess the meaning of company profitability by industrial origin.

One way out of this dilemma is to use Census data on the "overhead plus profit margin," obtained by subtracting out of sales, payrolls, and direct costs for materials and fuel. The margin is therefore made up of profits and such overhead costs as depreciation, advertising, research and development, and other indirect costs.

*Regional Share-of-Market Reports are now available as an online service of the Cybernetics Division of Control Data Corporation, which can offer many of the reports discussed in this chapter.

table 4-3
share of market report for sic 2051 bread, cake, and related products

Rank	Parent Company Branch Plants	Address	City	State	ZIP	Telephone Number	Estimated 1975 Sales ($ Million)	Share of Market (% U.S.)	Cumulated Share of Market
1	Intl. Telephone & Telegraph	320 Park Ave.	New York	N.Y.	10022	212-PL26000	1,011.5	11.07	11.07
	Continental Baking Co. Inc.	723 W. Capitol P.O. Box 829	Little Rock	Ar.	72203	501-3725166	10.1	.11	
	Continental Baking Co.	9340 Santa Monica Blvd.	Beverly Hills	Ca.	90210	213-2728024	32.3	.35	
	Continental Baking	6007 S. St. Andrews	Los Angeles	Ca.	90047	213-7533521	32.3	.35	
	Etc. . . .								
2	Campbell Taggart Inc.	6211 Lemmon Ave.	Dallas	Tx.	75221	214-3589211	539.9	5.96	17.03
	Colonial Baking Co. of Ala.	1110 S. Bell/Box 1806	Dothan	Al.	36301	205-7924131	3.2	.04	
	Merico Inc.	P.O. Bx 560	Fort Payne	Al.	35967	205-8454850	8.0	.09	
	Colonial Baking Co.	2200 Selma Hwy./Box 2774	Montgomery	Al.	36105	205-2883250	9.3	.10	
	Etc. . . .								
3	American Bakeries Co.	10 S. Riverside Pl.	Chicago	Il.	60606	312-4547400	465.8	5.13	22.16
	American Bread Co.	502 Cleveland Ave.	Attalla	Al.	35954	205-5385460	8.0	.09	
	American Bakeries Co. Inc.	P.O. Box 1279	Gadsden	Al.	35902	205-5385460	10.7	.12	
	Langendorf	7222 E. Gage Ave.	Los Angeles	Ca.	90040	213-7731923	13.9	.15	
	Etc. . . .								
4	Interstate Brands	12 E. Armour Blvd.	Kansas City	Mo.	64111	816-5616600	351.5	3.85	26.01
	Dolly Madison Cakes Div.	1101 N. 26th St.	Birmingham	Al.	35201	205-2523453	13.9	.15	
	Interstate Bakeries Corp.	P.O. Box 3905 Grand C	Glendale	Ca.	91201	213-8426183	11.6	.13	
	Weber Bkg. Co.	1955 Julian Ave. POB 13068	Glendale	Ca.	92113	714-2398155	9.3	.10	
	Interstate Brands C	2010 E. 15 St.	Los Angeles	Ca.	90031	213-7491337	.9	.01	
	Blue Seal Bread Div.	1010 46th St.	Oakland	Ca.	94608	415-4512433	9.3	.10	
	Etc. . . .								

In a study of 417 manufacturing industries in 1963, it has been demonstrated that the average gross margin (expressed as a percentage of total sales) was higher than 30.5% for industries with concentration ratios greater than 50% and less than 22.5% for industries with concentration ratios under 21%.[*]

Dr. John E. Kwoka, Jr., an economist with the Federal Trade Commission, has combined an ingenious use of such Census margin data and EIS data to throw new light on the significance of the 4-company concentration ratio and to suggest that the most meaningful measure of concentration would be a 2-company ratio.[†]

The choice of four as the lowest number of companies for which the Census Bureau could release data is dictated by the nondisclosure prohibitions under which the Bureau must operate in order to ensure response to Census questionnaires. It has of course long been recognized in the literature of industrial organization that while concentrated control of output power may confer power to set prices above competitive levels, much depends on who and how many control output and can therefore influence the strength of collusive or cooperative agreements.

By substituting the EIS Database for 1972 Census data, Kwoka first found the same basic correlations previously established in prior Census-based studies of the relation between 4-company concentration ratios and gross margins, after adjusting for the effect of high depreciation costs in capital intensive industries and for possible high advertising costs in consumer goods industries. But then he found that the correlations were even higher and more significant at the 2-company level, and the introduction of a third and fourth leading company in each industry had the effect of impairing the observed correlations. Kwoka concluded that non-competitive agreements or understandings are much more difficult to establish and maintain with three, four, or more companies than with two. Kwoka also offered a new and far more efficient definition of concentration. If the top two companies have 41% or more of total industry output (i.e. 26% or more for the first and 15% or more for the second), gross margins will generally rise to 32% as against an average for all manufacturing of 23%.

In Table 4–4 we have listed some 63 industries characterized by the latest EIS Database as having two-company concentration ratios of 40% or more.

[*] Norman R. Collins and Lee E. Preston, "Price-Cost Margins and Industry Structure," *Review of Economics and Statistics,* August 1969, p. 272.

[†] John E. Kwoka, Jr., "The Effect of Market Shares and Share Distribution on Industry Performance," Federal Trade Commission *Working Paper #2,* March 1977.

table 4–4
63 industries with 2-company concentration ratios greater than 40%

SIC	Industry	2-Company Concentration Ratio
2043	Cereal Breakfast Foods	59
2045	Blended & Prepared Flour	55
2046	Wet Corn Milling	57
2063	Beet Sugar	40
2066	Chocolate & Cocoa Products	56
2067	Chewing Gum	65
2095	Roasted Coffee	45
2111	Cigarettes	68
2121	Cigars	78
2131	Chewing & Smoking Tobacco	86
2296	Tire Cord & Fabric	44
2646	Pressed & Molded Pulp Goods	47
2771	Greeting Card Publishing	56
2813	Industrial Gases	42
2822	Synthetic Rubber	46
2823	Cellulosic Man-Made Fibers	58
2824	Organic Fibers, Non-cellulosic	51
2833	Medicinals & Botanicals	43
2841	Soap & Other Detergents	61
2892	Explosives	42
2895	Carbon Black	50
3011	Tires & Inner Tubes	43
3021	Rubber & Plastics Footwear	47
3031	Reclaimed Rubber	41
3211	Flat Glass	58
3221	Glass Containers	41
3229	Pressed & Blown Glass, nec	40
3275	Gypsum Products	57
3296	Mineral Wool	59
3313	Electrometallurgical Products	40
3332	Primary Lead	58
3333	Primary Zinc	58
3334	Primary Aluminum	58
3339	Primary Nonferrous metals, nec	47
3411	Metal Cans	43
3421	Cutlery	53
3465	Automotive Stampings	53
3482	Small Arms Ammunition	48
3483	Ammunition, exc. Small Arms, nec	54
3511	Turbines & Turbine Generator Sets	64
3534	Elevators & Moving Stairways	40

Continued

SIC	Industry	2-Company Concentration Ratio
3572	Typewriters	82
3573	Electronic Computing Equipment	41
3574	Calculating & Accounting Machines	61
3586	Measuring & Dispensing Pumps	49
3624	Carbon & Graphite Products	56
3632	Household Refrigerators & Freezers	58
3633	Household Laundry Equipment	57
3635	Household Vacuum Cleaners	54
3636	Sewing Machines	45
3641	Electric Lamps	53
3652	Phonograph Records	48
3661	Telephone & Telegraph Apparatus	76
3671	Electron Tubes, Receiving Types	55
3672	Cathode Ray Television Picture Tubes	48
3692	Primary Batteries, Dry & Wet	64
3694	Engine Electrical Equipment	46
3711	Motor Vehicles & Car Bodies	76
3724	Aircraft Engines & Engine Parts	60
3743	Railroad Equipment	49
3761	Guided Missiles & Space Vehicles	48
3764	Space Propulsion Units & Parts	57
3996	Hard Surface Floor Coverings	60

Dr. Kwoka has also used the EIS Database to investigate the nature of and reasons for the pattern of market shares commonly observed in manufacturing industries.* He has reached the conclusion that the search for general explanations, albeit a longstanding exercise in industrial organization, is futile. The reason is that the presumed regularity of size distributions is more apparent than real and there is an enormous diversity not captured by the theoretical distributions that have usually been postulated.

Dr. Kwoka has suggested that the EIS Database can illuminate the following additional problem areas in industrial organization research: (1) the investigation of the hypothesis that diversity of firm sizes in an industry contributes to technological progressiveness; (2) the examination of patterns of diversification and their effects on firm risk and profitability; (3) tracing over time the changes in size, shares, and rank of firms in an industry; and

*J. Kwoka, "The Diversity of Firm Size Distributions in Manufacturing Industries," Federal Trade Commission, Bureau of Economics Working Paper No. 12, February 1978.

(4) calculation of buyers' concentration ratios and relationships to profitability and sellers' market shares.*

In addition to the research purposes described above, Dr. Kwoka has summarized other uses of the EIS Database by both the Federal Trade Commission and the Department of Justice of interest in concentration analysis and antitrust litigation, as follows[†]:

The screening of mergers for possible anti-trust violations is facilitated by data on size and diversification of the affected firms. Evaluations of the merits of investigations at subsequent stages require progressively more detailed knowledge of market structures, often based on EIS data and supplemented by requested or subpoenaed figures. Periodic industry profiles are prepared using these data, for industries with on-going problems or special features deserving scrutiny. And data-gathering under other legislative authority uses EIS information to help identify major firms in specific industries or in the manufacturing sector as a whole.

Similar data requirements exist in private antitrust proceedings. Market definitions, market shares, descriptions of the firms involved, and identification of their actual and potential competitors are made possible with the EIS data. In their absence, the assembly of basic information is a difficult and time-consuming process.

vertical concentration

Another contribution that the EIS Database can make to the study of concentration is inherent in its ability to display the domestic sales of large companies broken down to all of their component markets, systematically defined at the 4-digit SIC level, as in Table 4–5, a so-called EIS Line of Business Report for ACF Industries, Inc. Such reports, available for all multimarket companies, are particularly useful for the analysis of vertical and conglomerate types of concentration.

A company is said to be seeking vertical concentration if it extends operations into two or more industries representing successive stages in the flow of goods or services from an earlier to a later stage of production or vice versa. "Forward vertical concentration" may characterize the extension of a company's activities if it is primarily engaged in early processing stages. A company

---

* Other investigators using the EIS Database to probe the relationship of profitability to industry characteristics include M. Gort and R. Singamsetti, "Concentration and Profit Rates: New Evidence on an Old Issue." *Explorations in Economic Research,* National Bureau of Economic Research, New York, v. 3, no. 1, 1976, pp. 1–20, and Timothy G. Sullivan, "The Cost of Capital and the Market Power of Firms," *Review of Economics and Statistics,* May 1978, pp. 209–17.

[†] John E. Kwoka, "EIS Market Share Data: Nature, Reliability, and Uses." Paper presented to the Anti-Trust Section meeting of the American Bar Association in New York on August 7, 1978, to be published in a forthcoming issue of the Anti-Trust Law Journal.

table 4–5
line of business report

Summary of Sales by Industry

ACF Industries Inc.   750 3rd Ave.   New York   N.Y.   10017

SIC	Industries in Which Company Operates	Annual Sales ($ Million)	% of Company Sales	Pct. of Industry Sales	Ranking Within Industry
3041	Rubber & Plastics Hose & Belting	29.7	4.64	3.55	7
3321	Gray Iron Foundries	8.9	1.39	.18	112
3429	Hardware, Nec.	2.6	.41	.08	288
3494	Valves & Pipe Fittings	60.5	9.45	1.22	13
3533	Oil Field Machinery	43.8	6.84	.82	31
3599	Machinery, Exc. Electrical, Nec.	2.8	.44	.01	275
3714	Motor Vehicle Parts & Accessories	150.2	23.47	.42	19
3743	Railroad Equipment	210.7	32.92	6.08	4
4743	Railroad Car Rental Without Svc.	89.0	13.90	7.15	5
5084	Industrial Machnry & Equip. Whlsng.	2.4	.37	.01	2,492
5088	Transportation Equip. Whlsng.	7.5	1.17	.16	33
	Total Manufacturing Sales	**509.2**	**79.55**		
	Total Nonmanufacturing Sales	**98.9**	**15.45**		
	Foreign/All Other Sales	**32.0**	**5.00**		
	Company Totals	**640.1**	**100.00**		

primarily engaged in later processing, or even in wholesaling or retailing, may want to move to "backward vertical concentration." A clear example is the ACF Incorporated "Line of Business Report," which shows that ACF, a major producer of railroad car equipment, is also heavily engaged in the leasing and rental of railroad cars.*

Antitrust agencies have long been sensitive to the extension of wholesaling and retailing operations on the part of major manufacturers of tires, glass, and other products. The term "dual distribution" was applied to the competition of integrated producers with their own fabricator, wholesaler, and retailer customers. Such instances of integration, backward or forward, are essentially "make or buy" decisions involving no obvious economies of scale, so that the impact of vertical concentration on competition is far from clear.

There are, of course, many other reasons for vertical integration, and the EIS Line of Business Reports will facilitate the analysis of integrated corporate operations, particularly with re-

*Such reports are also available from the Control Data online service.

spect to the particular way in which a company will choose to consolidate its operations.

In the consolidation of integrated activities, corporate accounting procedures tend to treat captive or subordinate operations as costs that will not appear as generating revenue. In the EIS estimates of company sales, on the other hand, all captive or subordinate establishments (for example, an auto company's captive foundry) will receive some allocation of total company sales. For such integrated manufacturers as paper, petroleum, and steel, an attempt is made to value at the market price the output of plants or mines engaged in early processing stages, and allocating to establishments classified in the later processing, transportation, and marketing industries a proportion of undistributed company sales.

Thus the EIS sales estimates for such integrated companies represent a hybrid valuation, falling short of the corresponding unconsolidated (and therefore duplicating) shipments figures carried in Census records, albeit in final agreement with total reported company sales.

This means that the EIS concentration ratios will tend to understate the corresponding Census ratios. A good example can be seen in the case of the 1972 Census 4-company ratio for SIC 3711 (Automobile Assembly—93%) and SIC 3714 (Automotive Parts—61%). Applying these ratios to total shipments of auto and parts produced in 1972 yields a figure for the top four companies of $51 billion, which is 25% higher than the consolidated figure of $41 billion reported by General Motors, Ford, Chrysler, and American Motors in their 10-K statements to the SEC and in their annual reports of automotive sales for the year 1972. EIS sales estimates, adjusted as they are to consolidated company sales totals, will reflect the same shortfall. It can be argued, of course, that Census concentration ratios actually overstate the true concentration for automotive parts by duplicating the automotive parts already embodied in assembled autos.

At any rate, by focusing on all integrated operations, the EIS Line of Business Reports can draw attention to important aspects of corporate activity that might otherwise be overlooked. Table 4–6 summarizes all the integrated petroleum markets in which the top eight oil companies operate. They are seen to account for $70 billion of sales in the production, refining, processing, transportation, and marketing of oil, gas, and petrochemicals. Such figures may not appear in annual reports as such, but they offer a more complete picture of the degree to which domestic petroleum operations are integrated. The top four companies have a 23% share and the top eight have a 37% share of the $190 billion total for all thirteen industries covering the domestic production and distribution of oil and gas and their major byproducts.

table 4–6
vertical concentration of leading u.s. oil companies, 1976 (selected sics)

SIC	Industry	Total Industry Sales ($ Million)	Top 4 Companies Sales ($ Million)	Top 4 Companies % of Total	Top 8 Companies Sales ($ Million)	Top 8 Companies % of Total
1311	Crude Oil & Gas	37,109.1	7,172.1	19.33	12,788.3	34.46
1321	Natural Gas	4,029.8	179.7	4.46	823.4	20.43
2821	Plastic Resins	13,565.3	1,028.5	7.58	1,394.1	10.28
2822	Synthetic Rubber	3,862.6	1,216.7	31.50	1,276.4	33.05
2911	Petroleum Refining	53,745.4	16,946.9	31.53	27,892.1	51.90
2992	Lubricating Oils	2,514.1	104.9	4.17	466.4	18.55
2999	Petroleum Products, nec.	724.6	83.3	11.50	194.3	26.81
4400	Water Transportation	3,252.8	501.4	15.41	501.4	15.41
4612	Oil Pipe Lines, Crude	4,398.4	1,176.3	26.74	2,267.3	51.55
4613	Oil Pipe Lines, Refined	2,004.6	496.0	24.74	866.6	43.23
5171	Petroleum Bulk Stations	22,214.1	5,381.8	24.23	8,192.7	36.88
5172	Other Oil Wholesaling	28,701.5	4,724.7	16.46	5,778.9	20.13
5541	Gas Service Stations	13,676.1	4,596.2	33.61	7,115.3	52.03
	Totals, Above 13 Industries	**189,798.4**	**43,608.5**	**22.98**	**69,557.2**	**36.65**

conglomerate concentration

According to Blair, conglomerate concentration can be defined as the possession of a share of a given industry's resources or activity by companies that are primarily engaged in other industries but are not suppliers or users of the given industry's products. In terms of market concentration, such shares become significant when the leaders achieve sufficient power to choose among alternative pricing policies, in which profits earned elsewhere may be used to subsidize sales at a loss for short periods. Because of high price-earnings ratios and favorable stock market conditions, the growth of large multiindustry companies reached a feverish tempo in the late '60s. Slower growth in the '70s may reflect public recognition that problems of conglomerate management remain difficult to resolve, and that greater profitability does not always result from conglomerate expansion.

There can be no question, however, that much of the concentration in American industry has been achieved by conglomerate mergers and acquisitions. At left is a list of eight large companies having plants in fifty or more 4-digit manufacturing industries.

One way to measure the degree to which conglomerate concentration is widespread is to record the concentration ratios for the 200 largest companies in each 4-digit manufacturing industry.

Company	Number of Industries with One or More Plants
Beatrice Foods	111
ITT	102
Gulf and Western	96
General Electric	88
Teledyne	86
Litton Industries	69
Tenneco	61
Jim Walter	56

Such a tabulation, not yet available from the 1972 Census, can be easily produced from the EIS Database and is shown in part as Table 4–7. Of the 430 industries, the top 200 companies account for at least 10% of total output in 80% of all industries, for more than 33% of output in about 40% of all industries, and for more than 50% in 25% of all industries (Table 4–8).

table 4–7

industries in which top 200 companies have more than 50% of sales, 1976

SIC	Industry	% of Sales, 1976
2032	Canned Specialties	50.4
2046	Wet Corn Milling	66.1
2079	Shortening & Cooking Oils	66.9
2095	Roasted Coffee	52.9
2111	Cigarettes	94.8
2121	Cigars	80.5
2132	Chewing & Smoking Tobacco	82.9
2296	Tire Cord & Fabric	82.2
2611	Pulp Mills	51.2
2631	Paperboard Mills	53.7
2654	Sanitary Food Containers	62.4
2812	Alkalies & Chlorine	52.2
2816	Inorganic Pigments	54.3
2821	Plastics Materials & Resins	69.9
2822	Synthetic Rubber	89.8
2823	Cellulosic Man-Made Fibers	59.2
2824	Organic Fibers, Non-cellulosic	80.9
2841	Soap & Other Detergents	65.1
2869	Industrial Organic Chemicals, nec.	66.2
2879	Agricultural Chemicals, nec.	50.2
2911	Petroleum Refining	78.7
2992	Lubricating Oils & Greases	55.2
3011	Tires & Inner Tubes	70.7
3211	Flat Glass	54.0
3312	Blast Furnaces & Steel Mills	66.4
3334	Primary Aluminum	62.2
3339	Primary Nonferrous Metals	57.1
3353	Aluminum Sheet, Plate & Foil	51.6
3411	Metal Cans	52.1
3465	Automotive Stampings	71.4
3511	Turbines & Turbine Generator Sets	81.1
3572	Typewriters	82.1
3573	Electronic Computing Equipment	62.9
3574	Calculating & Accounting Machines	71.5
3632	Household Refrigerators & Freezers	52.1

Continued

SIC	Industry	% of Sales, 1976
3641	Electric Lamps	70.9
3652	Phonograph Records	56.3
3661	Telephone & Telegraph Apparatus	83.8
3671	Electron Tubes, Receiving Type	87.0
3672	Cathode Ray Television Picture Tubes	73.0
3711	Motor Vehicles & Car Bodies	91.3
3714	Motor Vehicle Parts & Accessories	55.5
3721	Aircraft	69.4
3724	Aircraft Engines & Engine Parts	74.1
3731	Shipbuilding & Repairing	55.8
3743	Railroad Equipment	67.9
3761	Guided Missiles & Space Vehicles	88.2
3795	Tanks & Tank Components	62.4
3861	Photographic Equipment & Supplies	52.3

table 4–8
frequency distribution of concentration ratios
of top 200 companies in 449 manufacturing industries

Range of Concentration Ratios	Frequency	% of Total
Zero	34	7.6
Under 10%	157	35.0
10.0 to 19.9	90	20.0
20.0 to 29.9	54	12.0
30.0 to 39.9	43	9.6
40.0 to 49.9	22	4.9
50.0 to 59.9	18	4.0
60.0 to 69.9	12	2.7
70.0 to 79.9	7	1.6
80.0 to 89.9	10	2.2
90.0 to 99.9	2	0.4
Total	**449**	**100.0**

the eis database and financial analysis

EIS Line of Business Reports facilitate the calculation of a weighted average share of market estimate for every multi-SIC company. For multi-SIC public companies, for which periodic data on profit rates, price-earnings ratios, net worth, etc., are carried in financial databases, such information can be updated quarterly.

It therefore becomes possible to establish statistical correlations between profitability measures and share of market estimates, growth trends, advertising expenditures, and capital barriers to market entry. Past studies have demonstrated the existence of such relationships, based on very small numbers of companies for which adequate share of market estimates could be secured.[*]

Thus if m_1 represents a company's share in the first of n markets, and if c_1 represents the company's corresponding percentage of total domestic sales, then $\sum_1^n m_1 c_1$ will yield the weighted average company share of market. Such a measure could be confined to vertically integrated industries, if vertical concentration were the variable under study. For conglomerate companies, measures of diversification can be devised, based on those market shares that fall below the company average, to see whether diversification makes a positive or negative contribution to profitability.

Certainly for some 1,500 companies whose securities are traded on the major stock exchanges, if not for most public companies, the systematic examination of such regression relationships can yield many instances in which a company's reported profit rate or price-earnings ratios will fall below the "predicted" value and may therefore be presumed to be worth further exploration as an interesting speculation.

foreign concentration

The extensive conglomerate type of expansion of large companies over the past two decades was far outshadowed by huge rates of expansion abroad, so that the term multinational or transnational is now used to characterize large companies.

Official U.S. government data go back only to 1966, when special Census queries were sent to some 300 companies with majority interests in about 5,000 foreign affiliates. In the ten-year period 1966–1976, sales of such foreign affiliates quintupled, from $98 billion to $500 billion, reflecting in part the drastic price inflation brought on by the OPEC oil crisis in 1973.[†]

Excluding petroleum, which makes up about 40% of the total, the remaining foreign sales quadrupled in this period, also far outstripping domestic sales. EIS Line of Business Reports offer estimates of such foreign sales for about 250 companies, as a research by-product of the task of securing a domestic sales control total for each public company. Table 4–9 tabulates the leading

[*] Cf. William G. Shepherd, "The Elements of Market Structure," *Review of Economics and Statistics,* Harvard University, February 1972, pp. 25–37.

[†] William K. Chung, "Sales by Majority-Owned Foreign Affiliates of U.S. Companies," *Survey of Current Business,* May 1976, p. 25.

twenty American multinationals, ranked in the order of foreign sales.

The top twenty companies are seen to account for $133 billion of foreign sales—or 40% of the total sales of these companies. According to Table 2–2 foreign sales of the top 200 companies totaled $229 billion, and for the top 1,000 companies the total was $300 billion in the 1975–1976 period, when the *Survey of Current Business* study estimates foreign sales to have reached the $500 billion level. It is clear that the Database allocations of foreign sales are either too low for the leading companies, or else there are far more than 250 companies for whom foreign sales were significant. Still the Database figures on foreign sales are revealing, particularly in light of the fact that such sales are growing at twice the rate of domestic sales. It suggests that for the leading companies the sales of the foreign subsidiaries may soon outrank the domestic markets, as is now the case for such companies as Exxon, IBM, Gulf Oil, and Xerox. Further refinements in these foreign sales estimates can come when and if Database techniques are applied to the public records available abroad.

table 4–9
top 20 companies in foreign sales, 1976 ($ Billion)

Rank	Company	Total Sales	Foreign Sales	Foreign % of Total
1	Exxon	48.8	27.8	57
2	General Motors Corp.	47.2	15.1	32
3	Texaco Inc.	26.9	10.8	40
4	Mobil Corp.	27.5	9.6	35
5	Gulf Oil Corp.	16.8	8.4	50
6	Ford Motor Co.	28.8	8.4	29
7	International Business Machines	16.3	8.0	49
8	Standard Oil of Indiana	12.7	5.7	45
9	Standard Oil of California	20.6	5.5	27
10	Chrysler Corp.	15.5	5.2	34
11	International Telephone & Telegraph	11.8	4.7	40
12	Atlantic Richfield	8.9	4.4	49
13	Engelhard Minerals & Chemicals	6.5	3.0	46
14	Continental Oil Co.	8.4	2.6	31
15	Dow Chemical Co.	5.7	2.5	18
16	Xerox Corp.	4.3	2.3	53
17	Union Carbide Corp.	6.3	2.2	35
18	International Harvester	5.5	2.2	40
19	Goodyear Tire & Rubber	5.8	2.1	36
20	Phillips Petroleum	5.8	2.1	36
	Total	**330.1**	**132.6**	**40**

chapter 5

potential database uses by government agencies

Most government agencies involved in the regulation of business activity have found database access useful to one degree or another. In addition about a dozen federal agencies have found it desirable to develop specialized input/output databases that help solve problems in analysis, administration, or planning. Some noteworthy examples of such databases, both in current use and some that have been prepared for future use, are discussed below.

analysis of energy and environmental problems

Input/output analysis can perhaps make its greatest contribution in its ability to analyze the interrelationships among all the many components of the energy and environmental crisis of our times. An input/output model can be used to test the costs and feasibility of various options and thus contribute to a national debate and a resultant national energy plan, backed by a true consensus of public opinion. It appears that any national energy policy will involve higher costs and many sacrifices, along with huge subsidies by the government (and by taxpayers), comparable in magnitude to the many billions of federal funds invested in nuclear energy to date. But so far there has been no scientific attempt to assemble into a single model all the bits of information already in our possession that would truly validate the choice of any one set of energy programs over the long run. The need for such information system has been graphically described by Dr. Barry Commoner:

> If we wish to understand why the United States production system makes such shockingly inefficient use of energy—as a prelude to doing something about it—we need to understand not only the design of the various energy devices and of the instruments of production that they drive but also how each of these machines is used and how all of them might fit into the production system. Where. in that system, does it make sense to use a furnace, a diesel engine, a heat pump, an electric motor, an electric heater? What energy relationships call for the design of a new instrument or a different pattern of production? What economic considerations—which, after all, govern the design of the production system—have so consistently imposed on that system features that drastically curtail its thermodynamic efficiency?
>
> To answer these questions, we would need a kind of encyclopedia of production, a detailed catalogue of production processes in agriculture, industry, and transportation, and of their various productivities—what we put into them in the form of labor, capital, energy, and other resources relative to what they produce. Such a catalogue does not now exist, but various useful fragments are available.
>
> Some of them—such as the input-output tables that give the dollar value of certain contributions made by one production sector to another—have been created by economists in the last twenty or thirty years. Just recently, physical scientists concerned with resource problems have made more detailed estimates—chiefly based only on the First Law of Thermodynamics, however—of the amounts of energy used in agricultural processes relative to their output. But these are merely small beginnings on a monumental task.[*]

We confront an energy crisis, as do other countries, for which energy needs are based on fossil fuels, insofar as oil and natural gas reserves worldwide may last only a few more decades. Coal reserves will perhaps last for centuries, but coal is not by any means an easily accessible and cheap resource. The United States reached peak oil and gas production levels in the '60s, and is today increasingly dependent on uncertain high-priced foreign supplies.

As we saw in Chapter 3, productivity growth in the postwar years has been greatest in those industries characterized by heavy capital investment. These same industries, however, are also those most heavily dependent on cheap fuel and will therefore face increasing pressures on profitability as the costs of energy mount in the future.

[*] Cf. Barry Commoner, *The Poverty of Power* (New York: Alfred A. Knopf, 1976), p. 146.

The problem posed by the energy crisis can be stated in input/ output terms as follows: Given our current resources of manpower, fuel, and capital, what levels of output of energy among all producers, and what levels of consumption among all users of energy, will satisfy most requirements at maximum levels and at lowest costs, with the smallest detrimental impact on the environment?

Although energy and environmental problems are still handled by separate government agencies, there is increasing evidence of a close relationship between environmental pollution and high-energy systems, in accordance with the laws of thermodynamics. Every major type of environmental degradation of our air and water supplies can be viewed as the result of the inexorable increase in entropy or "disorder" that must accompany the transformations of energy in high-energy systems. Thus the chemical pollution of our waterways by industry and by modern farming technology results in the main from the massive use of a wide range of synthetic by-products of the process of converting fossil fuels to other forms of energy along with the production of petrochemical feedstocks. In tracing the transformations of fossil fuels in a modern high-energy system, we must regard their final emergence as environmental pollutants, and the cost of their control by society, as costs to be debited to our energy accounts.

In the same way the thermal pollution of waterways by coal-burning or nuclear power stations, along with associated emissions into the atmosphere, also involve hidden costs that are inextricably interwoven with the natural laws that govern energy transformations.

An energy input/output model can be adapted to test the environmental impacts of shifts in energy sources and uses, so that we need not speculate in the abstract about the relationships between energy and the environment. Federal regulatory agencies have in recent years supported the development of input/ output models to simulate energy flows and the Environmental Protection Agency has developed a Pollution Control Input/Output Model. But so far there has been no attempt to integrate the two models into one, despite the availability of many expert technicians and research agencies fully equipped to construct such an integrated model.*

* There are at least five private research agencies that have developed input/output models capable of simulating energy and pollution flows in the U.S. economy, aside from many capable economists employed in government agencies and the Department of Commerce. They are A.D. Little of Cambridge, Massachusetts; Battelle Memorial Labs of Columbus, Ohio; Jack Faucett Associates of Washington,. D.C.; the Research Triangle Institute of North Carolina; and Professor Anne Carter's unit at Brandeis University.

Environmentalists have asserted that we "waste" most of our energy input when the latter is judged by the standards of the Second Law of Thermodynamics. Thus by the substitution of energy inputs properly matched to the requirements of each type of demand, we may be able to achieve a high degree of conservation, at the same time eliminating environmental damage associated, for example, with the burning of fossil fuels or uranium at excessively high temperature merely to heat homes and provide hot water.

An input/output model constructed along the lines suggested by Dr. Commoner to test various assumptions on the substitution of energy sources would probably consist of a set of highly detailed input/output models and interrelated databases, in each of which the U.S. economy would be represented by about 700 sectors, corresponding to the 4-digit level of SIC detail. The master model would consist of the standard set of about 700 sector "equations" in which the output of each sector would be expressed in dollars as the sum of the sales of each sector to all other sectors. Such a model when "inverted" (i.e., when the 700 equations are "solved" simultaneously by computer) is now widely used by many government agencies for projections into the future.

The master model would then be interfaced with a series of special-purpose databases, constructed at the same degree of detail, containing a wide range of information on energy use and potential environmental pollution. There now exists, thanks to the Census Bureau, sufficient data to construct for each sector current estimates on energy use by type of fuel, in physical units or dollars, along with current prices, horsepower of prime movers in place, pollution coefficients associated with each type of fuel, water intake and discharge, freight tonnage originating by type of transport, etc. Such a database would permit feeding into the input/output model countless assumptions designed to answer a wide range of "what if" kinds of questions.

These models and databases can also be tied into another model that can trace the flow of capital investment to all sectors, as well as the capital investment required for each type of production of energy. Along with the correlations noted between high capital investment, energy use, and labor productivity there are disturbing signs that the productivity of additional units of capital and energy is now declining, judging from the fears expressed by the utilities and other energy sectors that they may not be able to generate enough capital to meet future energy requirements. If so, we would want to build into our input/output models the capability of testing the impact on energy use and output of alternative combinations of capital investment.

Table 5–1 lists those sectors representing the ultimate users of gross energy inputs in the U.S. economy of 1975. Industry is seen to account for more than one-third, followed by Transportation, and by the combined Residential and Commercial sectors, with about one-quarter for each. Note too that 18% of gross energy input is consumed, or rather wasted, as conversion loss. This reflects the fact that nearly two-thirds of the BTU content of fuel burned by the electrical utilities is lost in the process of conversion and transmission of electricity. It does not account for the inefficient use of energy by Second Law standards.

The U.S. Bureau of Mines has projected our gross energy requirements for future years, based on a total in 1975 of 71.1 quadrillion BTUs (see Table 5–2). These projections must be regarded as extremely optimistic. It assumes that we can nearly triple our coal production by the year 2000, but without considering the massive environmental impact, or even whether there are the necessary water supplies in the western strip-mining areas that would have to be so heavily exploited. Similarly the indicated 25-fold increase in nuclear power is mind-boggling in its implications for safety and radioactive waste disposal. And the projected

table 5–1
input of energy in the u.s., 1975

	Quadrillion BTUs	% of Total
Industry	**24.3**	**33.8**
Process steam	9.1	12.6
Direct heat	6.2	8.6
Electric drive	4.2	5.8
Nonfuel use (Petrochemicals)	4.2	5.8
Electrolytic Process	0.7	1.0
Transportation	**18.5**	**25.8**
Autos	10.0	13.9
Trucks	3.6	5.0
Buses	0.2	0.3
Motorcycles, etc.	0.1	0.1
Farm tractors	0.9	1.3
Airplanes	2.0	2.8
Railroads	0.7	1.0
Shipping	0.8	1.1
Fuel pipelines	0.2	0.2
Residential & Commercial	**16.2**	**22.5**
Conversion losses	**12.7**	**17.7**
Total	**71.7**	**100.0**

table 5–2
energy input projections, 1970–2000, by energy source (quadrillion btu's)

	1970	1975	1980	1985	2000
Coal	12.7	13.4	17.2	21.3	34.8
Petroleum	29.5	32.7	41.0	46.4	56.9
Domestic Supply	22.1	20.1	24.0	30.1	33.1
Imports, Shale Oil, etc.	7.4	12.6	17.0	16.3	23.8
Natural Gas	22.0	20.2	20.6	20.1	19.6
Domestic Supply	21.2	19.2	19.5	18.8	17.0
Imports	.8	1.0	1.1	1.3	2.6
Nuclear Power	.2	1.7	4.5	11.8	46.1
Hydropower, geothermal	2.6	3.2	3.8	3.9	6.0
Totals	**67.1**	**71.1**	**87.1**	**103.5**	**163.4**

Source: U.S. Bureau of Mines, "U.S. Energy through the Year 2000"

doubling of American imports of petroleum from abroad makes no allowance for the claims of other countries on this declining resource.

Nevertheless, any set of projections does serve the useful purpose of posing the problems, and it will undoubtedly take many years of public discussion and debate before we know the full range of options open to us. While it may be presumptuous to offer any precise scenarios for the future, there are certain energy strategies whose relative value can be tested by input/output models.

There are many quantitative parameters about which we simply do not have sufficient information as yet. For example, we do not have reliable governmental estimates of the extent of our domestic oil and gas reserves, nor do we know the true capital and operational costs of our present nuclear energy program. Of course it is too early, with the meager research to date, to assess the costs of alternate energy resources. But an energy input/output model will help rate energy programs on the basis of data or assumptions of varying degrees of reliability, and offer some notion of the confidence limits appropriate for any proposed energy strategy.

One crucial issue that should be examined and debated revolves around the economies of fuel use that may come from shifting to a more decentralized system. Coal and oil-burning public utility central stations apparently reach their highest fuel efficiency limits if they can conserve about 40% of the BTU content of the fuel converted to electricity for transmissions to the end-user. But it is well known that large industrial users can make even more efficient use of the fuel they burn themselves by better utilization of waste heat for space heating and refrigeration. This is why public utilities often justify lower rates offered to large industrial users, whose purchase of electricity often rests on a delicately poised "make or buy" decision. Alternate electric power pricing policies can be tested therefore on an energy input/output model that may favor greater industrial use for internal power generation at the expense of purchased electricity.

In 1975, for example, of the 26 quadrillion BTUs used by industry, about eight "quads" were associated with the purchase of about 600 billion KWH of electricity, which would yield only two "quads" of BTUs at the point of use.

Since 1973, large industrial users of energy have effected considerable improvements in energy conservation and fuel use. Conservation clearly must play an important role in our national energy planning: the precise conservation targets can themselves be subject to input/output analysis.

Perhaps the most significant gains in energy conservation can be made in the Transportation sector. Note from Table 5–1 that autos, trucks, and airplanes account for 21% of the gross energy input in BTU terms in 1975. But railroads with a mere 0.7% of the energy share are eight times more efficient, in terms of BTUs per freight-mile, than airplanes, and more than four times as efficient as trucks. In terms of BTUs required per passenger-mile, buses are five times more efficient than airplanes or cars, and mass transit would be at least twice as efficient in moving passengers.* Greater reliance on railroads, buses, and mass transit would require shifts in capital investment, so that an input/output Transportation model could help in the necessary phasing of such a massive alteration in our current use of transportation modes.

database applications

Database studies can play a subordinate but useful role in assessing the impact of the changes discussed above, by identifying the corporate protagonists most directly affected. It turns out that the top companies include not only the major suppliers of energy but also the major users of energy, and those whose operations generate the bulk of our environmental problems.

*Eric Hirst, "Energy Intensiveness of Passenger and Freight Transport Modes, 1950–1970," Oak Ridge National Laboratory, April 1973.

Databases have been prepared for various government and private agencies, which carry estimates for all manufacturing firms of the consumption of fuel and energy, air emissions from the industrial burning of coal and oil, water intake and discharge, and the movement of freight tonnage by mode of transport. All of these are activities for which the Census Bureau can offer statistical summaries by industry and region, and which when translated into database form exhibit extreme concentration with respect to the dominant position of the top 2,500 companies. It may be useful to review some of the details on how these databases are constructed, for they involve some necessary adjustments that have not yet been considered.

The various fuel components are in the long run somewhat substitutable, so that while the industrial need for energy is a function of technology, the regional mix of fuels required by an industry is subject to variation. Table 5–3, for example, lists the fuel requirements per employee for the Cement industry (SIC 3241), which is a particularly heavy consumer of energy. The industry overall fuel input per employee is twenty-two times heavier than that for all industrial establishments in terms of KWH equivalent, but there are variations in the degree of intensity of use between distillate fuel oil (thirteen times heavier) and coal (six times heavier) with respect to national totals.

Cement plants are generally located in areas with ready access to fuel supplies. Very few are found, for example, in the New England states, a region that must import the bulk of its fuel from elsewhere, and those few will probably substitute oil or coal for natural gas, since oil and coal can be more cheaply imported into New England than natural gas.

table 5–3
consumption of fuel and energy by the cement industry (sic 3241), 1971

	Cement Industry		Total Industrial
	Consumption (thousands)	Per Employee	Consumption Per Employee
Fuel Oil (Bbl.)	6,808	242	15
Residual Fuel Oil	4,632	165	9
Distillate Fuel Oil	2,177	77	6
Coal (short tons)	6,876	244	4
Natural Gas (000 cubic feet)	201,700	7,174	388
Total Fuel & Energy (000 KWH)	**125,900**	**4,478**	**199**

table 5–4
top twenty companies, consumption of fuel, excluding purchase of electricity

Rank	Company	Fuel (mil. KWH equivalent)	Number of Plants	% of Total
1	U.S. Steel Co.	83.7	103	2.5
2	Texaco	75.8	26	2.3
3	E.I. duPont de Nemours	56.6	80	1.7
4	Dow Chemical Co.	56.0	56	1.7
5	Shell Oil Co.	49.6	29	1.5
6	Gulf Oil Corp.	49.4	39	1.5
7	Union Carbide Corp.	48.6	127	1.5
8	Bethlehem Steel Corp.	46.5	61	1.4
9	Exxon	43.0	32	1.3
10	Republic Steel Corp.	40.8	43	1.2
11	General Motors Corp.	37.9	130	1.1
12	International Paper Co.	36.7	88	1.1
13	Mobil Oil Corp.	32.8	49	1.0
14	Standard Oil Co. of Indiana	30.6	26	0.9
15	Armco Steel	26.1	58	0.8
16	LTV Corp.	25.7	84	0.8
17	Phillips Petroleum	24.8	44	0.7
18	Allied Chemical Corp.	23.6	92	0.7
19	Kaiser Industrial Corp.	22.8	86	0.7
20	Alcoa	22.7	39	0.7
	Totals			
	Top 20	835.6	1,292	25.2
	Top 200	2,113.1	10,500	63.6
	Top 2,500	2,898.5	52,400	87.2
	All Manufacturing	3,322.4	112,207	100.0

Hence database estimates of inputs of each fuel should be adjusted to conform with fuel input totals reported by the Census Bureau for each state to reflect regional variation in the available supply of each fuel component.

Such state fuel input totals are available at the 2-digit level of SIC detail. In the case of the cement industry, the initial database estimates for two cement plants in Maine will provide for some natural gas input based on the national cement requirement of 7,174,000 cubic feet per employee. The Census, however, reported no natural gas consumption for all Maine plants classified in SIC 32, Stone, Clay and Glass Products, so that the computer programs must make a final adjustment that will eliminate the natural gas allocation for any cement plants in Maine, but will correspondingly boost the initial oil and coal requirements for the two cement plants in Maine.

In a similar way, by use of the appropriate state control totals embodied in the computer programs, the database estimates can now reflect much of the regional variation implicit in the establishment data collected by the Census Bureau for fuel consumption. Water use data, as collected by the Census Bureau, is also heavily affected by regional variation in water supplies, and similar adjustments have been used in the development of a database of water use.

Tables 5–4 and 5–5 demonstrate the degree of corporate concentration in the consumption of fuel and water. The top twenty fuel consumers, with 1,292 plants, account for 25% of all fuel consumed in manufacturing, while the top twenty water users, with 797 plants, account for 32% of all water used in manufactur-

table 5–5
top 20 companies, water discharged

Rank	Company	Water Discharged (Bil. Gallons)	Number of Plants	% of Total
1	U.S. Steel Co.	601.1	71	4.2
2	Bethlehem Steel Corp.	502.1	17	3.6
3	International Paper Co.	320.7	38	2.3
4	E.I. duPont de Nemours	247.5	67	1.8
5	Republic Steel Corp.	206.5	22	1.5
6	Texaco Inc.	192.4	23	1.4
7	Scott Paper Co.	190.9	16	1.4
8	Champion International Inc.	189.1	40	1.3
9	Shell Oil Co.	183.9	20	1.3
10	Weyerhaeuser Co. Inc.	182.5	20	1.3
11	Gulf & Western Industries	175.4	50	1.2
12	Dow Chemical Co.	174.0	58	1.2
13	National Steel	173.1	13	1.2
14	Inland Steel	165.5	5	1.2
15	Exxon	163.1	32	1.2
16	Armco Steel	151.3	29	1.1
17	Mobil Corp.	149.5	66	1.1
18	Georgia Pacific Corp.	145.7	88	1.0
19	Allied Chemical Corp.	142.9	77	1.0
20	LTV Corp.	137.2	45	1.0
	Totals			
	Top 20	**4,455.2**	**797**	**31.5**
	Top 200	**11,272.4**	**6,300**	**79.7**
	Top 2,500	**13,521.2**	**15,010**	**95.6**
	All Manufacturing	**14,143.5**	**26,342**	**100.0**

ing. In these tables we also show, as measures of concentration, the relevant percentages accounted for by the top 2,500 consuming companies. It is interesting to note that the top ten oil and steel companies appear in both listings, as evidence of the fact that petroleum refining and steel production draw heavily on both fuel and water supplies.

Water use appears to be somewhat more heavily concentrated than fuel consumption. The top 200 companies use 80% of all water, as against 64% of all fuel used in manufacturing. Similarly the top 2,500 companies use 96% of all water, and 87% of all fuel.

Broadly speaking, the listing of top users of fuel could also be taken to represent those companies whose fuel use can give rise to maximum potential atmospheric pollution.* It cannot be too heavily stressed, however, that all these database estimates are inferences with respect to possible or potential sources of industrial pollution, which do not by themselves take into account the actual pollution control measures already in place at the various fuel-burning locations.

Most of the companies included in the top 2,500 fuel burners also appear among the top users of water and would probably be found among the top users of pollution-control equipment. This is so because almost all such companies fall into the family of process-control industries discussed in Chapter 3. Some additional insights into these companies are provided by Tables 5–6 and 5–7, showing companies that lead in capital expenditures on process-control plant and equipment (which is increasingly designed to grapple with pollution abatement) and those that lead in the consumption of industrial chemicals. These tables demonstrate the same degree of corporate concentration shown by the two preceding tables, and both focus on the key role of the large chemical and paper companies that, along with the oil and primary metals companies, are the heaviest users of both energy and pollution-control equipment.

industrial exposure to carcinogens

Consumers of industrial chemicals are becoming aware of another environmental problem of increasing concern: the exposure of their workers to toxic materials, some of which, like asbestos, are carcinogens whose full impact will take many years to emerge. A database similar to that recording the consumption of

---

* In practice separate potential emission databases have been developed for users of coal, oil, and natural gas, based on sample EPA studies of the relationship of particulate emissions to various types of fuel. Such databases are useful in the marketing of various types of pollution-control equipment.

table 5–6

top 20 companies, annual capital expenditures on process control plant and equipment

Rank	Company	Expend-itures (Mil. $)	Number of Plants	% of Total
1	E.I. duPont de Nemours	585.5	62	3.9
2	Monsanto	214.2	42	1.4
3	International Paper Co.	191.3	33	1.3
4	Dow Chemical Co.	157.5	44	1.1
5	Allied Chemical Co.	154.4	76	1.0
6	Union Carbide Corp.	150.7	90	1.0
7	Celanese Corp.	138.7	33	.9
8	Proctor and Gamble Co.	129.7	32	.8
9	Atlantic Richfield	113.9	52	.8
10	Weyerhaueser	112.1	14	.8
11	Hercules Inc.	102.0	49	.7
12	Exxon	101.0	27	.7
13	Eastman Kodak	95.0	7	.7
14	American Cyanamid Co. Inc.	94.3	45	.7
15	Alcoa	94.2	28	.6
16	Champion International	90.7	16	.6
17	Mobil Corp.	89.9	71	.6
18	Scott Paper Co.	89.3	15	.6
19	Gulf & Western Industries	84.4	34	.6
20	Shell Oil Co.	83.1	29	.6
Totals				
Top 20		**2,946.8**	**752**	**19.9**
Top 200		**8,633.1**	**6,271**	**58.3**
Top 2,500		**12,749.8**	**14,771**	**86.1**
All Manufacturing		**14,808.1**	**24,440**	**100.0**

industrial chemicals can be developed, which can serve as a fruitful frame of reference for industry-wide epidemiological studies of the relationship between occupational illness and toxic materials used in the industry.

Table 5–9 lists twenty-two toxic materials for which the National Institute of Occupational Safety and Health has authorized industry-wide epidemiological research studies.* It would be possible, of course, to expand this list many times to include the hundreds of materials now suspected to have possible carcinogenic or toxic effects on industrial workers.

The exposure of industrial workers to a toxic material can come not only at locations at which the material is manufactured, but at

* The President's Report on Occupational Safety and Health, Annual Report 1973, pp. 136–146.

all locations at which the material in question is handled, reprocessed, or otherwise "consumed." Input/output analysis seeks to trace the flow of materials from the points of origin to the points of consumption and can be adapted to measure exposure rates at successive stages of fabrication.

For each material under investigation it would be necessary for the input/output analyst to assemble a complete listing of all the industries in which the material is produced, processed, reprocessed, or otherwise handled. It is also possible in this endeavor to systematize and quantify the magnitude of the physical volumes of each material produced and consumed, along with the number of workers exposed to each material in each producing and consuming industry. Heavy concentration of toxic materials per worker could then serve to set up priorities in the investigation of the implications to occupational safety and health.

table 5–7
top 20 companies, consumption of industrial chemicals

Rank	Company	Consumption (Mil. $)	Number of Plants	% of Total
1	E.I. duPont de Nemours	1,514	72	4.2
2	Goodyear Tire & Rubber	667	41	1.9
3	Dow Chemical Co.	620	41	1.7
4	Monsanto	611	57	1.6
5	Union Carbide Corp.	583	125	1.4
6	Firestone Tire & Rubber	512	37	1.3
7	Exxon	471	32	1.2
8	Eastman Kodak	446	12	1.2
9	Allied Chemical	423	81	1.1
10	Uniroyal	408	40	1.1
11	Proctor & Gamble Co.	397	29	1.1
12	U.S. Steel Corp.	393	79	1.0
13	General Motors Corp.	386	98	1.0
14	General Electric Co.	353	82	.9
15	Celanese Corp.	342	35	.9
16	B.F. Goodrich Co.	330	31	.9
17	Hercules Inc.	317	56	.9
18	American Cyanamid Co.	307	50	.7
19	Shell Oil Co.	263	28	.7
20	Texaco Inc.	255	26	.6
	Totals			
	Top 20	**9,598**	**1,052**	**26.6**
	Top 200	**22,587**	**6,044**	**62.6**
	Top 2,500	**31,571**	**15,394**	**87.5**
	All Manufacturing	**36,081**	**34,305**	**100.0**

Finally, such arrays of systematized, quantified data can lend themselves to quick and inexpensive computerized access as a Database of Toxic Materials. In constructing such a database in input/output terms, it would be necessary to array all the toxic materials along the vertical axis of a two-dimensional input/output grid with a summary column carrying quantitative estimates of the total volume of each material produced or consumed in the U.S. economy in a given year.

The "deliveries" of the material to each industry would be indicated along each row. There could probably be as many as 600 or 700 industries defined at the 4-digit level of SIC detail representing each column. If we conceive of a rectangular matrix with 300 suspect materials and 700 consuming industries, we have a total of 210,000 cells. Each cell would contain estimates of the volume of consumption of each material in each industry. The sum of estimates in any column represents the total physical volume of suspect materials required as "inputs" for that industry. Each

table 5–8
toxic materials now subject to industry-wide epidemiological research

Material	Industry or Occupational Group Under Study
Alumina	Aluminum refineries
Arsenic trioxides	Copper smelters
Asbestos	Sheet metal workers, asbestos plants, talc mines
Bauxite	Aluminum refineries
Benzidene	Dye manufacturing plants
Beryllium	Beryllium plants
Cadmium	Cadmium smelters
Carbon monoxide	Aluminum refineries
Chromic acid	Plating plants
Coal tars	Steel plants, aluminum refineries
Cotton dust	Cotton textiles plants, mattress workers
Cutting oils	Machine tool operators
Fiber glass	Sheet metal workers, fiberglass plants
Fluorides	Aluminum refineries
Iron oxide dusts	Gray iron foundries
Nitroglycerin	Munition plants
Potash fumes	Potash miners
Radon daughters	Uranium mines, other mining industries
Silica	Gray iron foundries, talc mining, brick manufacturing
Sulfur dioxide	Copper smelters, aluminum
Thorium 230	Uranium mines
Wood dust	Woodworkers

table 5–9

ten industries with highest rates of reported occupational illness

SIC	Name of Industry	Rate Per 100 Workers
3691	Storage batteries	3.8
3471	Metal plating	2.1
3629	Electrical industrial apparatus	2.1
3949	Sporting goods	1.8
3339	Primary nonferrous metals, nec	1.8
3356	Nonferrous rolling and drawing	1.6
3585	Refrigeration machinery	1.5
1929	Ammunition	1.4
3341	Secondary nonferrous products	1.4
3562	Ball and roller bearings	1.4
	Average rate, all manufacturing industries	**0.6**
	Average rate, all private industries	**0.4**

Source: "Occupational Injuries and Illnesses in the U.S. by Industry, 1973," BLS Bulletin 1874, Table I.

of these "inputs" can be associated, of course, with the number of production workers in that industry to focus attention on large ratios of consumption or exposure per worker.

The collection of data in this form is subject to the discipline imposed by the necessity of balancing the reported output of each material with all the estimated "inputs." If the consumption of a given material in any one industry is large, such consumption may have been reported in Census of Manufactures tables of purchased materials, or can be ascertained in other ways. The smaller the volume of a material consumed in an industry, the more difficult it would be to secure "hard" estimates of consumption. In such cases, input/output statisticians employ various allocation procedures in order to account for the total recorded output.

We shall choose one material to illustrate how such a database can be constructed, and how some additional insights can be gained by interfacing it with other computerized files. Inorganic lead, although not included in Table 5–8, has long been identified by the Occupational Health and Safety Commission as one of the five most serious industrial health hazards, along with carbon monoxide, silica, asbestos, and cotton dust.

It is interesting to note that the Bureau of Labor Statistics Office of Occupational Safety and Health Act publishes an annual summary of the recordable occupational illness incidence rates for every industry in the private sector. The tabulation for the year 1973 indicates that in that year the average incidence rate for all

table 5–10
partial list, major lead consuming industries, 1973

SIC	Industry Name	Lead Consumption (Th. Lbs.)	Employ- ment	Lead Consumed Lbs. per Employee
1961	Small arms ammunition	125,990	15,019	8,389
2791	Typesetting	25,000	15,392	1,624
3357	Nonferrous wire drawing	59,574	65,947	903
3411	Metal cans	18,260	66,909	273
3432	Plumbing fittings	11,020	21,613	510
3496	Collapsible tubes	10,000	4,351	2,298
3661	Telephone apparatus	15,033	130,427	115
3691	Storage batteries	1,562,035	18,627	83,859
3717	Motor vehicles	31,845	733,633	43
3731, 2	Ship building, boat building	25,000	137,000	185
3949	Sporting and athletic goods	12,067	47,690	253

private industries was 4 per 1,000 workers, and 6 per 1,000 in all manufacturing industries. No occupational illness rate was reported for SIC 3332 (Primary Lead), presumably because of lack of coverage. (There were only sixteen plants producing primary lead according to the 1972 Census of Manufactures.) The highest single recorded occupational illness rate (38 per 1,000), however, was reported for SIC 3691 (Storage Batteries), which is clearly associated with the industry's high reported consumption of lead, as the prime material input required for that industry (see Table 5–9).

If lead were to appear as a row in a database of toxic materials, we would begin with a figure derived from Census data indicating that the output of primary lead in 1973 was of the order of 1,600,000 short tons, of which 700,000 short tons was produced in SIC 3332 (Primary Lead), and 900,000 short tons was produced by secondary refiners, i.e., SIC 3341. These figures would be entered in the columns for these industries for the purpose of calculating exposure rates per worker in these producing industries. It is now also necessary to account for a corresponding consumption of 1.6 million short tons among all other "consuming" industries.

Since lead is a basic industrial material in wide use, there are as many as 170 industries whose consumption can be calculated in significant degree. One industry, SIC 3691, Storage Batteries, accounted for more than 700,000 short tons of lead consumption, or close to 70%, and about two dozen more industries accounted for much of the remaining consumption of lead used in the manufacture of ammunition, bearings, cable coverings, casting metals, collapsible tubes, foils, pipes, traps and bends, solder, terne and type metal, pigments, gasoline additives, weights and ballasts, as well as lead used in annealing and galvanizing.

Concentrations of materials consumption can be evaluated in terms of the number of production employees exposed to the material at each location in those industries that require the material as an essential input.

Table 5–10 is a partial listing of lead-consuming industries, the number of employees in plants with more than twenty employees in those industries, an estimate of lead consumption (in pounds) for that industry, and a calculated ratio of lead consumption per employee. Sometimes, as in the case of SIC 2791, Typesetting, even though the consumption of lead is not very great—on the order of 25 million pounds—because the number of workers in typesetting establishments is relatively low, the degree of exposure per worker may be quite high—of the order of 1,600 pounds per worker. On the other hand, the automotive industry has a relatively large lead consumption, but spread among 733,000 employees, the exposure rate per employee is not high.

By permitting computer programs to multiply these industry-wide consumption ratios by the employment estimates carried in the Database for each establishment, it is possible to secure initial estimates of worker exposure at each establishment based on the assumption that in each industry the degree of exposure from plant to plant bears a direct relationship to employment. This in turn derives from the basic assumption made in input/output economics that all establishments classified in an industry, defined at the most detailed level possible, share a common technology of production.

In reality, of course, plant technologies in each industry will vary with the age of equipment installed, as well as a host of other factors associated with regional variations as well as changes in local employment practices. Most important, the Database estimates of exposure, based purely on inference, cannot initially account for any environmental controls already adopted by plant managers. The chief function of the Database, however, is to serve as a repository for the information on the actual plant situation that must be collected from field surveys directed to each location whose potential exposure to a toxic material appears large enough to warrant such direct surveys.

In industrial marketing, for example, such computerized estimates of potential consumption are used to direct a company's sales and promotional efforts in the most efficient manner. Agencies charged with the enforcement of environmental controls can use the Database to direct their mail and telephone inquiries to key locations in a systematic way, input information derived from responses back into the Database, and periodically analyze the impact of regulatory policy by company, industry, and geographic areas.

The emphasis in the use of a Database for such a purpose must be on the voluntary cooperation of both buying and selling companies with the regulatory agencies, for the removal of environmental hazards is crucial to the long-term viability of all the companies concerned.

database uses in national and regional planning

Shortages of energy and other materials, coinciding with continuing high rates of inflation and unemployment, have in recent years heightened interest in legislative proposals to improve the ability of the government to formulate programs to ensure balanced growth. Unless problems of shortages, inflation, and unemployment fade away, the mounting pressures behind these proposals will some day bear fruit. If so, input/output and database analysis can play a useful role in the coordination and study of the information on which sound growth policies can be based. Database studies can also help extend public participation in the federal policy-making process, by affording an opportunity for all to perceive in advance the consequences of proposed policies in specific terms.

The way in which Congress and the President might be able to arrive at effective, balanced economic growth policies has been spelled out by the Advisory Committee on National Growth Policy Processes in its report "Forging America's Future."* The Committee tried to answer the question raised in recent public opinion polls on why people felt that "government is no longer up to carrying out its assigned task."

The short answer is a simple one. Our nation and the world have changed since 1960, but our government has not kept pace. Governmental institutions and processes have not responded to changes in the envi-

---

*The Advisory Committee was established in January 1976 as an expression of Congressional fears that the nation was in danger of running out of resources. Its report, issued in early 1977, and reprinted in full in the January/February issue of *Challenge* magazine, is remarkable in the degree of agreement reached on certain key recommendations, despite the wide diversity of political and economic interests represented by the members.

ronment that they are supposed to understand and manage. We are backing into the future, stumbling as we go.

There are two major developments that have altered the condition of the United States; our nation has not fully recognized them, nor has our government adequately reacted to them. The first is the accelerating interdependence of the nations of the world (despite increased nationalism and often poor cooperation) and the effects of this on a United States economy committed—in theory, if not in practice—to free-market principles. The second is the almost unmarked but rapid shift of our already mature industrial civilization into a new phase of industrial and societal development. Together these have produced a host of new problems that tax our government's capacity to understand, let alone deal with them.

The Committee sees the American economy today as the product of a "postindustrial revolution" with as profound an impact as the industrial revolution of 200 years ago, or the agricultural revolution in the dawn of recorded history. Whereas previous revolutions transformed the economic base from hunting and fishing to farming and then to industry, with ten-fold gains in per capita income at each advance, postindustrial society offers far fewer comparable gains in labor productivity.

In 1947, half of the labor force in the United States was engaged in producing goods. In 1980, two-thirds of the labor force will work in the nonindustrial sectors: utilities, trades, finance, service, and government. These are low-profit (or nonprofit) sectors, with little opportunity to employ capital (except in the utilities) in increasing labor productivity. As we have noted elsewhere, these sectors (again with the exception of the power and transportation utilities) are not characterized by corporate organization precisely because of the limited opportunities for capital investment and profitability.

The Committee sees in the growing corporate concentration in industry and energy supply the reasons for a decline in the influence of market forces, requiring increasing government intervention. But perhaps the most important aspect of the postindustrial revolution is the growing interdependence of sectors and regions, which according to the Committee is "a function of the complexity of society and specialization within it. Not too long ago, problems tended to be contained within a city, then a state, then a nation. Now, almost everything in the world is related to everything else."

It is this interdependence that renders so ineffective the government's attempts to arbitrate disputes that cannot (or should not) be resolved in the market place. The Committee offers several notable instances where government intervention proved to be contradictory and self-canceling.

The huge wheat sales to the Soviet Union in 1973 resulted in Russian bread made from American wheat, transported halfway around the world, costing half as much as American bread at home.

Again, birthrate statistics on the postwar "baby boom" suggested there would be a shortage of elementary schools and teachers in the 1950s, to be followed by corresponding shortages in secondary schools and colleges in the '60s. At each stage the government undertook teacher education and construction programs after the fact and failed to terminate them in time, so that most of the 1.2 million teachers graduating by 1980 will not get teaching jobs!

Perhaps the largest example of government intervention was the interstate highway program first proposed in the early '50s as a "planned" network of expressways to link all regions of the nation. That program is substantially completed, but in hindsight we now see that it expanded truck and car transport enormously at the expense of other transport modes that are far more efficient in the use of energy. The program set off an unplanned "urban sprawl" that accelerated the decline of central cities, and exacerbated the associated problems of welfare, crime, and poverty.

The Committee concludes with a grim recital of the now familiar contradictions of a national energy policy increasingly dependent on foreign petroleum, with the government not even in possession of independent data on domestic oil supplies:

The lesson to be learned is that there is need for both a mechanism to collect data of greater integrity, and for multiple centers of data generation and analysis. The data and information bases which underlie national planning efforts should not be colored by their devout hopes for certain future conditions. We need data that are gathered in a consistent fashion, treated with integrity, and made available to all parts of the government as well as to the private sector.

Since the government must intervene, it should do so as well as possible, and for this the Committee recommends that the Congress and the President consider and respond to the periodic long-range analyses prepared by a National Growth and Development Commission, set up as an independent agency in the Executive Branch of the government. New policy-planning responsibilities will also be shared by the Joint Congressional Committee, the Council of Economic Advisors, the Office of Management and Budget, and a new intergovernmental organization that will supply the crucial links between national and regional planning.

Of particular interest is the Committee's recommendation for a Center for Statistical Policy and Analysis that will provide the technical framework for the Commission and for all other planning agencies by "developing a model of the American economy broken down by region and sector."

**database uses by
government agencies**

We have seen that sectoral analysis must play a key role in the development of a national energy policy capable of satisfying all industries. It will be immediately apparent that the models developed by the Center would tie in directly with those needed for the analysis of energy and environmental problems. In fact, any attempt to separate economic planning and the analysis of inflation from those of energy and the environment would be most artificial.

Perhaps the most important recommendation of the Committee is the expansion of the responsibilities of the present Advisory Commission on Intergovernmental Relation to assess, before the fact, the potential consequences of Federal action on states and localities. The Committee observes that:

In recent decades, the powers and responsibilities of the Federal government have become more and more enmeshed with those of state and local governments. Increasing Federal intervention in national economic affairs affects, and is affected by, the power of states to control land use, to set up local governments, to develop systems of taxation, and so on. The growth of environmental concerns and the emergence of important resource imbalances across regions has intensified this interdependence.

Such co-mingling of powers could not have been clearly envisioned by the drafters of the Constitution. Nor did the framers foresee that, once they were welded into a unified economic entity, regions would be increasingly sensitive to and dependent upon major national and international developments.

The Advisory Commission should therefore monitor and evaluate the regional impacts of existing policies and programs and take cognizance of the fact that:

the old industrial Northeastern and Great Lakes regions, for example, must now make painful economic adjustments as the advantages of location they once enjoyed become diluted by rising energy and production costs, and by the development of an efficient national network of communications and transportation. Many areas of the Southeast and Southwest, after decades of economic lag, now confront problems of burgeoning growth, partly because they are exporters of energy to other, less fortunate regions. The upper Great Plains and the Wyoming Basin face environmental disruption, increased demands for water, and population growth in areas now short of water and sparsely populated.

To meet the needs of regional analysis, the Center for Statistical Policy will have to assume the gargantuan task of collecting sufficient data to construct regional input/output models that will interface with the master national model, a task that the Committee feels will provide few economies of scale:

Thus, a model which seeks to divide the United States into ten regions and to examine the movement of commodities among them, or the effects of particular national policies on each, requires ten times the data, collected at roughly ten times the cost of a model which seeks to portray the aggregate economy.

In this regard I believe that database access to establishment records can greatly facilitate this admittedly laborious data-collection effort in the construction of regional models, particularly if university research bureaus can be involved in a collective, standardized effort, perhaps under the supervision of federal agencies. Several regional input/output models were attempted in the 1960s, with small grants from the Economic Development Agency in the Johnson Administration. Insufficient interest in how such models could be used, plus serious deficiencies in data collection, rendered them ineffective, however.

In the construction of a regional input/output model that would interface with a national model, it is important that all the detailed regional inputs and outputs are distinguished with respect to whether they are exports to or imports from other regions, on the one hand, or foreign exports or imports on the other. In building a national model, input/output statisticians have on hand detailed data on foreign exports and imports, but no equivalent body of such data exists for regions, although the 1972 Census of Transportation does provide the basic framework for analyzing much of the interregional movement of manufactured goods.*

Another difficulty is that strict adherence to Census data would leave many regional transactions blank if they are dominated by too few establishments to warrant Census publication under the Census Bureau's nondisclosure rules.

Database access can help solve both problems. University research teams, as nongovernmental agencies, can conduct the necessary mail or telephone surveys in each area to secure the desired information without being bound by Census Bureau restrictions. In accordance with the facts of economic concentration, of the 300,000 plus business establishments that account for the bulk of the U.S. private Gross National Product, surveys directed to no more than 50,000 or 60,000 establishments would be required to secure the information necessary to complete the regional models. For each of ten regions, say, surveys of 6,000 establishments would not seem too heavy a burden, particularly with the opportunity of using graduate students who can secure professional training in the preparation and analysis of the returns.

Regional development commissions are now using database printouts to analyze the economic base of specified areas in order to attract new industries, so that the sponsorship of university research along these lines would seem a logical adjunct to the

*See Appendix C, "On The Construction of Regional Input/Output Tables," p. 121.

work of the proposed Center for Statistical Policy and the Advisory Committee on Intergovernmental Relations.

Such a program would require an expansion of current curricular offerings in regional economics, economic geography, and input/output analysis. The great emphasis in these regional studies on the operations of identified establishments and firms, particularly those that have a dominating influence in local economies, can be regarded as a truly democratic extension of public participation in the governmental policy-making process.

The Advisory Committee sees this public participation as so important that they recommend that:

responsible public participation in policy-making that affects national growth and development be encouraged by providing for public access at each stage of the process. Tax deductions should be permitted for moderate contributions to membership organizations seeking to influence government decisions, and direct financial assistance should be given to groups which could otherwise not be heard.

Easy public database access to information on the relative roles of large companies in the workings of the American economy can also make a modest but helpful contribution to enlisting public support for sound national policy decisions.

appendix a   bibliography on input/output

The international literature on input/output is so voluminous that the United Nations Statistical Office has published many volumes of bibliographic references covering the period 1955–1970. The following books will provide useful expositions on both introductory and more advanced levels:

Almon, Clopper et al. *1985: Interindustry Forecasts of the American Economy*. Lexington, Mass.: Lexington Books, 1974.

Barna, Tibor, ed. *Structural Interdependence and Economic Development*. New York: St. Martin's Press, 1963. (Proceedings of the Third International Conference on Input/Output Techniques)

Blitzer, Charles, R., Peter B. Clarke, and Lance Taylor, eds. *Economy-Wide Models and Development Planning*. New York: Oxford University Press, 1975.

Carter, Anne P. *Structural Change in the American Economy*. Cambridge, Mass.: Harvard University Press, 1970.

Carter, Anne P. and Andrew Brody. *Applications of Input/Output Analysis*. Amsterdam: North-Holland Publishing Co., 1970.

Chenery, Hollis B. and Paul Clark. *Interindustry Economics*. New York: Wiley, 1959.

Leontief, Wassily W. *Input/Output Economics*. New York: Oxford University Press, 1966.

**input/output
databases**

Leontief, Wassily W. et al. *The Future of the World Economy*. United Nations, 1976

Leontief, Wassily W. et al. *Studies in the Structure of the American Economy*. New York: Oxford University Press, 1953.

Miernyk, William W. *Simulating Regional Economic Development*. Lexington, Mass.: Lexington Books, 1970.

Polenske, Karen R. and Jiri V. Skolka, eds. *Advances in Input/Output Analysis*. Cambridge, Mass.: Ballinger Publishing Co., 1976. (Proceedings of the Sixth International Conference on Input/Output Techniques)

Yan, Chiou Shuang. *Introduction to Input/Output Economics*. New York: Holt, Rinehart and Winston, 1969.

appendix b listing of input/output databases

An input/output database can be generated by interfacing an establishment database properly coded at the 4-digit SIC level with a row of technical coefficients, taken from a detailed input/output table. Several hundred rows of technical coefficients, defined at the 4-digit SIC level, may be found in the Department of Commerce publication "Input/Output Structure of the U.S. Economy: 1967," Volume I, *Transactions Data for Detailed Industries* (1974). The following listing includes many products and services coded to 4-, 5-, 6-, and 7-digits of SIC detail, for which Economic Information Systems, Inc. maintains annual sets of transactions estimates, each of which can generate listings of intermediate purchases of the given product or service by major firms and establishments.

Although the estimates of government input/output statisticians provide a frame of reference for all these products and services, some of them, such as "fluid power components" or "pollution control equipment," represent product families that cut across many different standard industrial classifications. Many manufacturers of equipment and components, in preparing their technical brochures and catalogues, may not be able to trace the specific SIC classes in which their product line will fall. Nevertheless, if a determination can be made of the industrial function served by the product line, it will generally be possible to establish the relative importance of most of the 4-digit industries that would be potential purchasers of the product line, and then adjust these purchasing "weights" to an overall market size that can be reconciled with Census Bureau statistics on output. In this way, a set of technical coefficients can be determined even for products not covered by specific SIC codes.

SIC	PRODUCT
20	**FOOD**
20115	Lard
20231	Dry milk products
202312C	Casein, caseinates
20261	Bulk milk & cream
2034	Dried & dehydrated fruits & vegetables
20411	Industrial flour
2046	Corn syrup, starches & feed
2062-3	Cane & beet sugar
2074	Cottonseed oil & by-products
2075	Soybean oil & by-products
20761	Linseed oil & by-products
2077	Animal fats, oils & by-products
2087	Flavorings
22 & 23	**TEXTILES & APPAREL**
2211	Cotton fabrics
2221	Synthetic & silk fabrics
2231	Wool fabrics
2241	Narrow fabrics
2257,8	Knit fabrics
2281	Yarn, cotton & synthetics
2283	Wool yarn
2284	Thread
2291	Felt goods
2293	Padding & upholstery filling
2295	Coated, laminated fabrics
2296	Tire cord & fabrics
2298	Cordage & twine
2393	Textile bags
2394	Canvas products
2395	Pleating & stitching
2399W	Webbing tiedowns, slings & fittings
24	**LUMBER & WOOD**
2421	Sawmill products
24262-84	Industrial hardwood stock
2435	Hardwood veneer & plywood
2436	Softwood veneer & plywood

SIC	PRODUCT
2441,2+	Nailed & wirebound wooden boxes and crates
2448	Wood pallets & skids
2491	Wood preserving service
2492	Particleboard
26 & 27	**PAPER, PACKAGING & PRINTING**
2621F	Filter paper
2621P	Printing, writing papers
26212	Uncoated groundwood paper
26213	Coated printing and converting paper
26214	Uncoated book paper
26215	Bleached bristols
26412	Waxed and laminated papers
26413	Gummed tape
2642	Envelopes
26432S	Specialty bags
26432F	Film & foil combination bags
26432C	Cellophane bags
26432PE	Polyethelene bags
26432P	Paper pouches
26433	Paper shipping sacks
2645	Die cut paper, paperboard & cardboard
2645T	Tabulating cards
2651	Folding boxes
2652	Set-up boxes
2653	Corrugated boxes
2654	Sanitary food containers
26551	Fiber drums
265522	Fiber cans, composite cans
2655231	Fiber cores & tubes
2661	Building paper & board
275	Commercial printing
27515	Labels, tags
28/I	**INORGANIC CHEMICAL PRODUCTS**
28121	Chlorine
28122	Soda ash
28123	Caustic soda
28124	Caustic potash
2813	Industrial & process gases
2813W	Welding gases
28132	Acetylene

SIC	PRODUCT
28133	Carbon dioxide
281341	Inert gases: argon, helium, others
281344	Nitrogen
281345	Oxygen
2816	Inorganic pigments
28161	Titanium dioxide
281633	Iron oxides
28193	Sulfuric acid
281941+	Boric acid & borates (borax)
281943+	Chromium acids & compounds
281944	Hydrochloric acid
281946+	Fluorine & bromine acids & compounds
28195	Aluminum compounds: oxide, hydroxide, alums, other
281973+	Phosphates: Na, K, Ca
2819953+	Mercury & compounds
2819956+	Nickel compounds
2819958+	Phosphorous & compounds
2819965	Rare earth compounds
2819968+	Silica gel
2819971+	Silver compounds
2819975+	Sulphur compounds, nec
2819980+	Tin compounds
2819987+	Zinc compounds
2819994+	Industrial bleaches, inorganic
287313	Ammonia
287314,5	Ammonium compounds
28741	Phosphoric acid
287311	Nitric acid
2895	Carbon black
28991	Salt: evaporated, refined
1476	Rock salt
281974	Silicates
2819775	Silicon carbide, other compounds
281971	Potassium sulfate, other potassium compounds
28197S	Sodium chlorate, sulphides, hydrosulfide, sulfates, sulfites, hydrosulfite, other sodium compounds

SIC	PRODUCT
28198	Catalyst preparations
2819904	Barium compounds
281991-	Calcium carbonate, chloride, other calcium compounds
281992	Activated carbon
2819934	Copper oxide, sulfate, other copper compounds
2819939	Hydrogen peroxide
2819942+	Ferric chloride, other iron compounds, nec
2819948+	Magnesium compounds
2819950+	Manganese compounds
2819998-	Tungsten compounds
28/O	**ORGANIC CHEMICAL PRODUCTS**
28414+	Glycerine
2861	Gum and wood chemicals
286113+	Rosin & derivatives
286125	Charcoal: industrial use
286129	Tall oil
28651	Cyclic intermediates: basic petrochemicals and coal-tar products (benzene, toulene, etc.)
286910	Cyclic oxy-hydrocarbons: cyclic acids, acid salts, alcohols, aldehydes, ketones, esters, metallic esters, others
28691C	Chlorinated and other halogenated cyclics
28619N	Cyclic nitro-hydrocarbons
28692	Acyclic hydrocarbons & oxy-hydrocarbons: basic petro-chemicals, acids, acid salts, alcohols, glycols, aldehydes, ketones, esters, metallic esters, others
28692C	Chlorinated and other halogenated acyclics
28692N	Acyclic nitro-hydrocarbons, amines
28692S	Sulfonated, phosphated organics & metallic salts
28692F	Fatty acids & oil derivatives: fatty alcohols, amines, others
28732	Urea
28992	Fatty acids

SIC	PRODUCT	SIC	PRODUCT	SIC	PRODUCT	SIC	PRODUCT
28/P	**POLYMER PRODUCTS**	28695A	Other resin-product additives: antioxidants, heat stabilizers, UV absorbers	30413H	Hydraulic hose	**33**	**PRIMARY METAL PRODUCTS**
28213	Thermoplastic resins, total			3069	Fabricated rubber products		
282132	Polyethylene resins	28695C	Formulants: defoamers, thickeners, thinners, viscosity modifiers, tackifiers	30693	Sponge and foam rubber	3312	Iron & steel mill products
282135	Polypropylene & other olefin resins			30695	Mechanical rubber goods: molded, extruded	3312WR	Wire rod, total
		28695E	Enzymes			331221	Wire rod/carbon
282136	Styrenic resins: polystyrene SAN, ABS	28695F	Chemically modified fats, oils, fatty acids: sulfonated, phosphated, chlorinated	306951	Rubber & plastic sealing, insulating, packaging & joining tape	331223	Wire rod/alloy
282137	Polyvinylchloride & copolymer resins					331225	Wire rod/stainless
2821381	Acrylic resins	28695MS	Metallic soaps	30790S	Plastic strapping	33124P	Plate, total
2821385	Polyamide (nylon) resins	2869537+	Reagent & diagnostic chemicals	307906	Flexible plastic tubing	331241	Plate/carbon
2821389	Acetals, polycarbonates			30791	Plastic film & sheet: flexible	331243	Plate/alloy
28214	Thermosetting resins, total	286955	Commercial & specialty solvents, estractants; chlorinated & halogenated solvents, vapor phase degreasers	30791SH	Plastic shrink film & sheet	331245	Plate/stainless
282141,4	Melamine & urea formaldehyde resins			30792F	Foamed plastic products, flexible	33123	Sheet & strip, total
282142	Phenolic resins, tar-acid resins			30792R	Foamed plastic products, rigid: insulation, packaging materials, others	331231	Sheet & strip, hot rolled/ carbon
282143	Polyester resins & intermediates	2892+	Explosive products	30793, 61,2	Laminated & reinforced plastic sheet	331233	Sheet & strip, hot rolled/alloy
2821475	Epoxy resins & intermediates	2899C	Corrosion inhibitors			331235	Sheet & strip, hot rolled/ stainless
2821477	Urethane resins & intermediates: diisocyanates, polyols	28994	Gelatin, industrial	30793D	Decorative sheet, strip, tape: laminated plastic, plastic-foil	33123C	Sheet & strip, coated
		28995E	Essential oils			33123G	Sheet & strip, galvanized
2821E	Electrical insulating, potting, wire-coating resins	289953	Concrete & cement hardeners, grouts	30794	Rigid & semi-rigid containers, plastic	331671	Sheet & strip, cold rolled/ carbon
2822	Synthetic rubbers, rubber latexes	289954	Flotation agents, drilling specialties	307943	Plastic bottles	331673	Sheet & strip, cold rolled/alloy
2822NV	Non-vulcanizing (quick-cure) elastomers	2899559	Metal treating compounds: nitriding, pickling, heat-treating	307944	Plastic drums	331675	Sheet & strip, cold rolled/ stainless
285195	Organosols, plastisols			30795	Molded plastic products, industrial	33124B	Bar, total
2823,4	Synthetic fibers, total	2899561	Oil & fuel treating compounds			331242	Bar, hot rolled/carbon
28516,7	Industrial OEM coatings, finishes: synthetic resin preparations, lacquers, enamels, varnishes, gel coats	2899572	Recording-instrument inks	307965	Plastic pipe & fittings	331244	Bar, hot rolled/alloy
		2899577	Water & boiler treating compounds	30796E	Engineering plastic products: vessels, ducts, process equipment	331246	Bar, hot rolled/stainless
		289958	Waterproofing compounds			33168	Bar, cold finish/carbon
285161	Maintenance & shop-coat paints: rust proofings, severe-environment products, special primers	2899590	Synthetic lubricating, hydraulic, other industrial oils: see Group 29	30798,9	Plastic rod, tube	331681	Bar, cold finish/alloy
						331683	Bar, cold finish/stainless
		289959F	Fire-retardant chemicals & coatings	**31**	**LEATHER**	33124S	Structural shapes
2861653	Powder coatings	289959P	Plating specialties	3111	Tanned & finished leather	33176	Pipe & tube, total
285169	Synthetic-resin maintenance coatings: vessel liners, severe-environment coatings	289959X	Fluxes	31433	Protective footwear	331761	Pipe & tube, pressure/carbon
						3317643	Pipe & tube, pressure/alloy
2891	Adhesive preparations, synthetic adhesive resins	**29**	**PETROLEUM PRODUCTS**	**32**	**STONE, CLAY & GLASS**	3317661	Pipe & tube, pressure/ stainless
2891M	Adhesives: mechanical & structural use			32113	Flat glass & glass products	331762	Mechanical & structural tubing/carbon
2891P	Adhesives: packaging & flexible product use	2911EF	Engine fuels: industrial use	321142	Tempered glass products	3317645	Mechanical & structural tubing/alloy
		2911W	White oils	3221	Glass containers		
2891465	Hot-melt adhesives	29115	Specialty naphthas	32292	Lighting & electronic glassware	3317663	Mechanical & structural tubing/stainless
28915	Sealants, industrial	29116	Liquefied petroleum-refinery gases	32293	Glass fibers	33155	Wire, total
2899563	Sizes			32294	Industrial & technical glassware	331551	Wire/carbon
		291106+	Waxes & wax preparations			331553	Wire/alloy
28/S	**SPECIALTY CHEMICAL PRODUCTS**	29119	Asphalt: industrial use	3229425	Glass pipe, fittings & process equipment	331555	Wire/stainless
		2952	Asphalt & tar felts, boards	3251,9	Chemical (acid-resistant) brick	331221	Ingot & semi-finished shapes/ iron & carbon steel
28411+	Industrial cleaners	29921	Lubricating oils, greases	3255,97	Clay & non-clay refractories		
28411-	Mechanic's hand soaps	299221	Metal-cutting oils	3264	Porcelain/ceramic electrical products	331223	Ingot & semi-finished shapes/ alloy
28411M	Metal degreasers, cleaners	299222	Metal-rolling oils				
28424	Polishes, industrial	299223	Metal forming, drawing, extruding, spinning oils	326498+	Ferrites, electronic & other	33125	Ingot & semi-finished shapes/ stainless
28434,7	Textile assistants, finishes			32696	Ceramic process equipment		
28438	Surface-active agents: wetting, emulsifying, dispersing, foaming, detergency	299224	Grinding oils	3274	Lime	33124T	Tool steel
		299225	Heat treating, tempering, quenching oils	3291	Abrasive products, total	331S	Ferrous metal scrap
				32911C	Carbides: silicon, boron, tungsten	331211+	Coke: metallurgical & process use
2851651+	Paper, paperboard & textile coatings, impregnants	299226	Rust-proofing, slushing, coating oils	32911,4	Abrasive grains, grit, shot	3313	Electrometallurgical products: ferroalloys
		29923	Hydraulic oils	3291119	Aluminum oxide		
285995	Waxes	29924	Electrical insulating oils	32912	Bonded abrasive products	33152	Nails & staples
286931	Food & drug chemicals	29925	Heat transfer oils	32913	Coated abrasive products	33121,2	Iron castings, total
286931F	Fragrances, industrial odor chemicals	29927	Process & other specialty oils	32922F	Asbestos friction products	3321-	Gray iron castings
				32922I	Asbestos insulation products	33217,8	Cast iron pipe & fittings
286933,5	Plasticizers, rubber-processing chemicals	**30**	**PLASTICS & RUBBER**	32927	Asbestos-cement pipe, duct	3322	Malleable iron castings
				3293	Gaskets, packings & seals/ total	3324,5	Steel castings, total
		3011	Rubber tires, OEM			3324,5C	Steel castings/carbon steel
		302115	Protective rubber footwear	32932	Gaskets, gasket materials	3324,5A	Steel castings/alloy
		30411	Conveyor & elevator belting	32933P	Packings	3324,5S	Steel castings/stainless
		3041FT	Flat transmission (drive) belts	32933S	Seals	3361,2,9	Nonferrous castings, total
		3041NH	Non-hydraulic hose	3296	Glass fiber insulation	336D	Die castings, nonferrous
		3041PT	Positive-drive (timing) belts			3361	Aluminum & alloy castings
		3041VT	V-belts			3362	Copper & alloy (brass, bronze) castings
						33PMC	Powder metal castings, ferrous & nonferrous

SIC	PRODUCT	SIC	PRODUCT	SIC	PRODUCT	SIC	PRODUCT
3331	Primary copper & alloy products, total	342115,9	Shearing & cutting hand tools	**35**	**MACHINERY**	3565	Industrial patterns: foundry
333973	Magnesium products, mill shapes	3423T	Mechanics hand tools	3519	Internal combustion engines	35661,2	Geared speed reducers, increasers, drives, varidrives, transmissions
333974	Nickel products, mill shapes	342325	Machine knives, cutting dies	35191,2	Gasoline engines		
333976	Tin & alloy products	34251,3	Powersaw blades, wood & metal	35193	Diesel engines	35663	Gearmotors
333977+	Titanium products, mill shapes	3429	Hardware, OEM: locks, hinges, etc.	3532	Mining machinery	35664	Loose gears, pinions, racks
333LT	Lead-tin alloy products			35322	Crushing, pulverizing & screening machinery	3567	Metallurgical furnaces & ovens
333SB	Solder & brazing alloys: wire & paste	342982	Casters & wheels	3535	Conveyors & conveying equipment	356817	Plain bearings & bushings
333LC	Low-temperature casting alloys	34337C	Combustion equipment for solid & liquid wastes	3541	Machine tools, metal-cutting	356831	Packaged hydraulic drives, transmissions
334S	Nonferrous metal scrap	3441	Fabricated structural metalwork	3542	Machine tools, metal-forming	356831,2	Clutches, brakes & couplings: mechanical, electric, hydraulic; universal joints, flexible shafts
3339An	Antimony products			35441	Dies, tools, jigs & fixtures		
3339Ar	Arsenic products	3443T	Pressure & process vessels, storage tanks	35442	Industrial molds		
3339Be	Beryllium products	34431	Heat exchangers	35451	Cutting tools: twist drills, other	356833,4	Sprockets and sprocket chain
3339Bi	Bismuth products	34432	Platework, weldments			356835,6	Sheaves, pulleys
3339Co	Cobalt products	34433	Power boilers, process steam generators	35452	Precision measuring tools	3568391	Valve operators
3339Cr	Chromium products			35453	Machine-tool attachments	3568397	Mechanical shaft seals
3339Ga	Gallium products	344462	Sheetmetal bins, vans, hoppers, ductwork	3546	Power handtools: electric, pneumatic	3569FI	Fluid-power linear & rotary actuators, positioners
3339Ge	Germanium products	3451	Screw machine products	3547	Metal-mill machinery: rolling, tubemaking	3569F2	Fluid-power system accessories: intensifiers, boosters, accumulators, dampers, snubbers
3339Se	Selenium products	3452	Fasteners, total	35493	Gas welding & cutting equipment		
3339Si	High-purity silicon, epitaxial silicon	3452B	Bolts, studs				
		3452S	Screws: machine, cap, set, self-locking	35495D	Drawing machines	35691	Packing, packaging and package handling machinery
3339Ta	Tantalum products	3452T	Tapping screws	354952	Metalworking assembly machines	356912	Labeling & marking machines
3339Te	Tellurium products	3452W	Wood screws	3551	Food products machinery	356924	Filters & strainers, pipeline & OEM
3351	Rolled & drawn copper & alloys, total	345260	Rivets	35514	Food products packaging machines		
33513	Copper & alloy rod, bar	3462	Iron & steel forgings, total			3569246	Water and process filtration equipment
33514	Copper & alloy sheet, strip, plate	3462C	Carbon steel forgings	3552	Textile machinery		
		3462A	Alloy steel forgings	3553	Woodworking machinery	356993	Gas generators
33515	Copper & alloy pipe, tube	3462S	Stainless steel forgings	3554	Paper industry machinery	356995	Centrifuges & separators
33511	Copper & alloy wire, nonelectrical	3462Ch	Chain, forged & other	3555	Printing machinery & supplies	356999	Air (pneumatic) motors
3332	Primary lead & alloy products, mill shapes	3463	Nonferrous forgings, total	35591+	Chemical and petroleum machinery	3573P	Process & industrial control computers, sensor interfacing, input/output equipment, other peripherals
		34631	Aluminum & alloy forgings				
3333	Primary zinc products, mill shapes	346321	Copper & alloy forgings	35592	Foundry, die-casting machinery		
		3465,9	Metal stampings				
3334	Primary aluminum products, total	3466	Crowns, caps & closures	355925	Blast cleaning, tumbling, other finishing machines	3576	Industrial scales, weigh-batching systems
33347	Aluminum ingot, extrusion billet	3471	Plating & polishing services	35593,4	Plastics & rubber machinery	3585	Refrigeration & air conditioning equipment
		3479C	Metal coating services	3559581	Metal cleaning, degreasing, coating, drying, other finishing machinery		
33531,2	Aluminum sheet & plate	34791	Metal nameplates			35854	Refrigeration compressors
3354-,552	Aluminum rod, bar, shapes, structurals, mechanical tubing/total	34793	Galvanizing services			35892	Water treating equipment: softeners, chlorinators, ion-exchange units, others
		3493	Steel springs (except wire)	355959	Kilns, furnaces, ovens, lehrs		
		349411	Process control valves	3561	Industrial pumps, total		
33541,2	Aluminum extrusions: bar, shapes, mechanical tubing	349414	Regulator valves, filter-lubricator-regulators	35611P	Process centrifugal pumps	358928	Waste-treating equipment
				356117	Rotary-positive pumps	35893	Vacuum dust-abatement equipment
33542-	Aluminum pressure tubing	349416	Solenoid valves	356117P	Proportioning pumps		
33395	Precious metals: silver, gold, others	34942	Fluid-power valves	35612	Fluid-power and lube-oil pumps, hydro-power supply sets	35992	Fluid-power cylinders
		349431	Valves, pressure: iron, brass, bronze/total (gates, globes, checks)			35994	Flexible metal hose, tubing, bellows, diaphragms
333972	Cadmium products						
3357	Nonferrous insulated wire & cable, total			3562	Ball & roller bearings, total		
		349432	Valves: cast & forged steel	35621	Ball bearings	**36A**	**ELECTRICAL PRODUCTS**
33574	Communication wire & cable	349432S	Valves: stainless steel	35622,3	Roller bearings: tapered, cylindrical, needle, spherical		
33576,9	Insulated appliance wire, cords, leads	3494331	Ball valves			3612P	Power transformers
		3494333	Butterfly valves	3563	Air & gas compressors	36120	OEM transformers: control, signal, instrument, lighting
33577	Magnet wire	3494335+	Plug valves	356312	Vacuum pumps		
33578P	Power wire & cable, leads	3494339	Diaphragm & pinch valves	3564	Blowers & fans	3613A	Switchgear assemblies, circuit breakers
33578S	Insulated signal, control & electronic wire & cable	349435	Safety & relief valves	3564C	OEM unit-cooling & exhaust blowers, fans	3613-	Switchgear & power-circuit components, total
		349436	Steam traps, pressure				
3398	Metal heat treating	34945	Pipe fittings	356453,4	Air processing equipment: filtering, washing, drying, other	361332-	Electromagnetic & manual power switches, contactors
33991	Metal powders & pastes	34946	Tube & hose fittings, hydraulic hose assemblies			36134F	Fuses
				356465	Particulate emissions collectors: electrostatic precipitators, fabric filters, mechanical collectors, wet scrubbers	36137	Relays: electromagnetic, overload, time-delay
34	**FABRICATED METAL PRODUCTS**	3495	Wire springs				
		34961	Steel wire rope & cable, slings			3621	Motors & generators, total
3411	Metal cans	34964,5	Industrial screening, wire cloth, wire mesh			3621F	Fractional hp motors
34121	Metal pails	3497A	Aluminum foil: plain, coated, laminated			3621N	Integral hp motors
34122,3	Metal drums, barrels			356466	Gas & vapor emissions control equipment: scrubbers, absorbers, combustion (oxidation) equipment, adsorbers	3621S	Subfractional motors, gearmotors; instrument & control motors, generators
		34970	Other metal foil & leaf				
		34992	Collapsible metal tubes				
		34993	Metal strapping			3622	Industrial controls & control-circuit components, total
		3499455	Permanent magnets				
		3499461	Steel shipping boxes			3622P	Positioners (control system)
		3499475	Metal spools & reels				

SIC	PRODUCT
3622S	Specialty industrial controls, automation equipment: electric-electronic, transducer-encoder, programmable, digital & logic
3622W	Industrial web-process controls
362212+	Motor starters
362216	Motor control centers
36224P	Control panels & panel components
36224,7	NC machine-tool & other machine controls
362243	Limit switches, interval timers, other pilot-circuit, signal-circuit & control devices
362244	Pushbuttons, light-pushbuttons, pushbutton stations
36228	Rheostats, resistors
36229	Vari-speed drive controls
3623	Electric welding apparatus
36232	Welding electrode, stick & wire: carbon steel, alloy, stainless
3624	Carbon & graphite products
36291	Capacitors
36292	Rectifying, power-conversion apparatus; power supplies
362931	Coil windings
362933	Solenoids
3641	Electric lamps, OEM
3643C	Metal contacts, terminal blocks
3643S+	Switches: electrical & electronic
36438+	Wiring connectors, terminals & splicers: electrical & electronic
36442	Electrical conduit & fittings
3691	Storage batteries
3694	Engine electrical (ignition) equipment, harness sets

36B ELECTRONIC PRODUCTS

SIC	PRODUCT
362262C	Ultrasonic cleaning equipment
366262T	Ultrasonic metalworking tools: drills, solderers, welders
3671,3	Electron tubes
3674	Semiconductors & integrated circuits, total
3674LE	Light-emitting semiconductors, digital-display elements: LED's, others
3675LS	Light-sensitive (photoelectric) semiconductor elements
36741	Integrated circuits, semi-conductor networks
36742	Transistors
36743+	Diodes & rectifiers
3675	Capacitors, electronic
3676	Resistors, electronic
3677	Electronic transformers, coils, reactors, chokes
36791	Transducers, mechanical (strain, pressure), acoustical, optical
367918	Thermocouples, other thermal transducers

SIC	PRODUCT
36792	Electronic component packages, modules, integrated multicomponent circuits, circuitboards, subassemblies
36792L	Solid-state logic units, micro-processors
367933	Relays, electronic
36794	Electronic power supplies, converters
36795	Printed & etched circuits
36799C	Crystals, electronic
36799F	Filters, electronic
36933	Industrial x-ray equipment & supplies

38 INSTRUMENTS

SIC	PRODUCT
3811	Scientific & engineering instruments
3822	Automatic environmental & appliance control devices
38222	Temperature & pressure-responsive switches
3823	Process control instruments, total: on-stream monitoring & control of temperature, pressure, liquid-level, flow. Includes sensors, transmitters, indicators, recorders, controllers; analog & digital processors, interfacing & station equipment
3823G	Temperature & pressure gauges
38237A	On-stream analyzers: pH, gas, liquid
382344	Annunciators, alarm & signal equipment
38242	Integrating fluid meters
38243	Digital counting devices
3825	Electrical/electronic measuring & test instruments
38253-	OEM indicating & recording panel meters, analog & digital
38292	Physical testing & inspection equipment
38321	Analytical instruments
38321P	Pyrometers
38321S	Optical sensing, photovoltaic instruments & controls
38423	Industrial personal safety equipment
38435	Protective clothing
38614E	Engineering photo reproduction equipment & supplies
387316	Timing mechanisms & devices

39 MISCELLANEOUS MANUFACTURING

SIC	PRODUCT
3963	Buttons, apparel
3964	Needles, pins & apparel fasteners
39642	Zippers
3991-	Brushes

MINERALS

Antimony & compounds
Barite
Beryl, berryllium & alloys
Bismuth & alloys, compounds
Borax, boron compounds
Cadmium & compounds
Calcium & compounds

PRODUCT

Chromite, chromium & compounds
Clays & shales, total
Clays, Kaolin
Clays, ball
Clays, fire & stoneware
Clays, Bentonite
Clays, Fuller's earth
Cobalt & compounds
Diatomite
Feldspar
Fluorspar, cryolite, hydrofluoric acid
Gas, natural
Graphite, natural & manufactured
Industrial sands: foundry, glass, others
Iron ores & refined compounds: oxides
Lead & zinc ores, compounds
Lead & compounds
Limestone: broken, crushed & ground
Magnesium & alloys
Magnesia, dead-burned dolomite, magnesium compounds
Mercury & compounds
Mica, incl. built-up scrap
Molybdenum & compounds
Perlite
Potash, potassium compounds
Pumice
Rare earths & compounds
Salt, industrial
Sulfur
Talc, soapstone, pyrophyllite
Tin & alloys, compounds
Tungsten & alloys, compounds
Vermiculite
Zinc products

SERVICES

SIC	
4011	Rail Freight Services
4213	Motor Freight Services
4511-21	Air Freight Services
481	Data transmission services
4911	Electricity generation & transmission, non-residential
492	Gas transmission & distribution, non-residential
4941	Water supply, non-residential
631	Group life insurance
632	Group accident & health insurance
6331	Fire & casualty insurance, non-residential
7311	Advertising
7321	Direct mail advertising, industrial
7349	Cleaning & maintenance services, industrial
7361	Employment agency services
7362	Temporary help supply services
7372	Computer programming & other software services
7374	Data processing services
7392	Management, consulting & public relations services
7394	Equipment rental & leasing services
7397	Testing laboratory services
8911	Engineering & architectural services
8931	Accounting services

PRODUCT

PURCHASED FUEL & ENERGY

Purchased fuel, total
Fuel oil
Distillate oil
Residual oil
Coal
Coke & breeze
Gas
Other fuels
Purchased electric energy

POLLUTION CONTROL MEASURES

Dust collectors
Fuel particulates
Water intake
  Treated water
  For process use
  For air conditioning
  Steam, power generation
  Cooling, condensing
  Boiler feed, etc
Water discharged
  Through public utility sewer
  Surface waterbody
  Ground
  Transferred to other uses
Water treatment (intake)
  Total
  Aeration
  Coagulation & settling
  Filtration
  Softening
  Ion exchange
  Corrosion control
  PH
  Other
Water-waste (effluent) treatment
  Total
  Coagualtion & settling
  Filtration
  Activated sludge, digestion
  PH
  Chlorination
  Flotation
  Chemical treatment

TECHNICAL EMPLOYEES

Engineers
  Chemical
  Electrical, electronic
  Industrial
  Mechanical
  Other
Scientists
  Mathematicians
  Chemists
  Physicists
  Metallurgists
  Geologists
  Biologists
Technicians
  Draftsmen
  Electrical, electronic
  Industrial-mechanical

OTHER CENSUS MEASURES OF INDUSTRIAL ACTIVITY

Payrolls
Production workers: number, man-hours, wages
Value added
Total purchases
Capital expenditures for structures, machinery & equipment

appendix c   on the construction of regional input/output tables

A regional input/output table, even in the highly condensed format shown below, is ideally suited to defining the economic relationship of a region to the rest of the nation. At extreme levels of disaggregation, too detailed for reproduction here, such tables can illuminate the links between national and regional planning, by focusing attention on the quantitative measures of the region's exports and imports, or the relative mix between so-called "national" and "local" industries.

Regional economists often make a similar distinction between "basic" and those service industries required to support the "basic" industries, which are thought to bring outside income into the area. Increases in basic employment will require corresponding supportive expansion in nonbasic employment. Hence, most Chambers of Commerce and local planning agencies take pains to attract basic industries, assuming that local supporting services will be forthcoming.

In describing the difficulties faced by smaller communities in attracting new industries, it has been predicted that:

Only the clustering of many automated operations will provide the necessary supporting population. Further, more and more industries are clustering into mutually supporting complexes, based on input-output linkages, complementary labor demands, technological interactions, and so forth. Linked, individual firms cannot enter or leave their present location easily or unilaterally; therefore, an urban area finds it more difficult to attract independent firms. In sum, bigger, tighter-knit industrial complexes, larger and fewer manufacturing centers.*

We can, for illustration, use a highly summarized version of an input/output model for the state of Washington, for the year 1972, and based on research conducted by the Washington State Department of Commerce and Economic Development, and the Graduate School of Business Administration of the University of Washington.[†]

The 1972 study was based on a breakdown of the Washington economy into fifty-five sectors or industries. For purposes of simplification, we have aggregated about three dozen manufacturing industries into a single manufacturing sector, and five resource industries and nine service industries into a single nonmanufacturing sector. Yet even in this simplified form, the table yields some fundamental facts about the Washington economy.

Note first that the value added in all the intermediate and final sectors in the state adds to $19.2 billion, which can be taken as the state's gross product, analogous to the Gross National Product for all states. Thus, the Gross National Product can be viewed as the sum of each state's contribution to value added. But we can also arrive at a gross product on the expenditure side, by adding the total purchases of the household, government, and investment sectors: $12.0 billion plus $7.7 billion equals $19.7 billion.

This means that consumption of final users in the state exceeds the value created by regional producers by about $.5 billion, and that the state is therefore a net importer of goods and services from the rest of the economy. Another way to see this is to note that imports into the state total $9.8 billion, as against the state's exports of $9.2 billion.

In a balanced economy, of course, some states must be net importers and others will be exporters; but a region's exports are regarded by regional planners as most amenable to development or to the influence of exogenous factors. Let us examine, for example, in greater detail the components of the Washington export figure. As that portion of Washington's gross product that is consumed outside the state, it is generally dependent on eco-

---

*Wilber R. Thompson, *A Preface to Urban Economics* (Baltimore: Johns Hopkins Press, 1965).

†Regional input/output research reached a peak in the mid-60s, supported by funds from the Economic Development Administration, but Administration support declined sharply after 1968. Bibliographies of such projects are available from the Economic Development Administration of the Department of Commerce, and from the United Nations.

nomic factors operating at a national (or even international) level. Relatively unaffected by local factors, it is this portion of the regional activity that would be greatly dependent on planning decisions taken at the national level.

Among the three dozen manufacturing sectors accounting for $10.8 billion of total manufacturing sales, the aerospace industry, according to the study, accounted for $1.9 billion, of which about one-third was shipped to the federal government, one-third to other states, and the remainder to nations abroad. Obviously such large magnitudes would play a significant role in any set of national plans. Another notable fact is that these magnitudes reflect the operations in large part of a single enterprise, the Boeing Company. And here we come to an important difference between the techniques of constructing national input/output tables and those for regions. It would have been impossible for the authors of the Washington study to have constructed a meaningful table without information about the size and shipments of the several large Boeing plants in Washington, and without close study of the Boeing annual report and 10K statement, plus perhaps interviews with Boeing representatives. Such procedures are, by law, not available to the statisticians working on national input/output tables under federal auspices.

Thus, it should be clear that the construction of regional input/output models must be done by nongovernmental agencies that can operate without being bound by Census Bureau nondisclosure rules; but the number of large companies whose operations would so dominate regional activity is small. Database access to

two-sector input/output model for the state of washington, 1972 (millions of dollars)

	Intermediate Sales			Final Demand			
	Manu-facturing	Non-manufacturing	Intermediate Sales to Industries	Sales to House-holds	Sales to Government and for Investment	Exports	Total Sales
Manufacturing	1,356	818	2,174	1,030	1,557	6,053	10,813
Nonmanufacturing	1,511	2,223	3,734	6,078	2,176	3,194	15,182
Total Industry Purchases	2,867	3,041	5,908	7,108	3,733	9,247	39,012
Imports	3,460	1,578	5,038	3,284	1,453	—	9,775
Value Added	4,486	10,563	15,049	1,608	2,514	—	19,171
Total Purchases	10,813	15,182	25,996	12,000	7,700	9,247	54,940

Source: Philip J. Bourque, Richard S. Conway, Jr., The 1972 Washington Input/Output Study, Graduate School of Business Administration, University of Washington, June 1977

these relatively few companies would greatly facilitate the task of identifying and quantifying the shipments of such establishments, at least for the purpose of preparing preliminary estimates. A single set of DIALOG commands addressed to the Economic Information Systems Database would elicit the information that there were only eight aerospace plants in the state of Washington with over 100 employees, of which five belonged to the Boeing Company, with total shipments exceeding $1 billion.

We thus can see that the regional input/output analyst can enjoy a great advantage and can make a correspondingly more realistic contribution to the technique of gathering information on the impact of national change at regional levels. He can make direct inquiries by mail, phone, or interview to all large establishments in his area. Such direct inquiries can help modify estimates of regional input requirements, which in the absence of such data are generally assumed to follow national patterns. It is probably fair to state that the test of a true commitment to national planning would be the encouragement of regional studies for all areas carried out at the maximum degree of detail, care, and accuracy that is possible.

index